REMEMBER
OBSERVE
REJOICE

A Guide to the Jewish Feasts, Holidays, Memorial Days and Events

Petra van der Zande

Maps and photos: unless stated, photo's taken from the internet (public domain).
Graphic design: Petra van der Zande.
Published by: TsurTsina Publications Jerusalem, Israel.

Scripture references taken from the KJV - King James Version - public domain

ISBN 978 965 7542 67 5
Special KJV edition

Order information write to email:
tsurtsinapublications@gmail.com

Or log into website: http://www.Lulu.com or
www.tsurtsinapublications.com

Summary:
Reference guide about the when, why and how the Jewish Feasts, Holidays and Events were celebrated in ancient times, and in Israel today.

This is the story of a people which was scattered over all the world
And yet remained a single family; A nation which time and again
Was doomed to destruction, and yet, out of ruins, rose to new life.
Abba Kovner

**Abba Kovner
(1918-1987)**
Born in Lithuania, this Jewish Hebrew poet was also a writer and partisan leader. He became one of the great poets of modern Israel.

"And that the Gentiles might glorify God for his mercy; as it is written, For this cause I will confess to thee among the Gentiles, and sing unto thy name. And again he saith, Rejoice, ye Gentiles, with his people. And again, Praise the Lord, all ye Gentiles; and laud him, all ye people." **Romans 15: 9-11**

INTRODUCTION

There are many books on the market about the meaning and spiritual
significance of the Biblical Feasts

> **REMEMBER** His marvelous works. Psalm 105:5
> **OBSERVE** His statutes. Psalm 105:45
> **REJOICE (Praise)** in your salvation." Psalm 13:5

and the lessons Christians can learn from them. This publication is a simple guide to the Jewish Festivals, Holidays, Celebrations and Events a visitor to Israel may experience. It explains the why, when and how these events were observed in ancient times, and how it is done in Israel today.

Having returned to *Eretz Yisrael* from all corners of the earth, many communities continue to celebrate events in their own, special ways. In order to keep things 'simple', I have chosen to mainly describe the customs of the Ashkenazi community. Hebrew words are written in Italics, including the word Torah. In the glossary of terms you can find a short explanation of the words which are marked with an asterisk. (*)

An earlier publication, *A Christian Guide to the Jewish Festival of Sukkot,* gives more in-depth information on the 'what' and 'how' of the Feast of Tabernacles, and the Four Species in particular. *The Season of our Rejoicing,* soon to be published, will combine information from this book and the *Christian Guide.*

Simcha means "joy" or "rejoicing". The commandment to rejoice, a basic element in Jewish religious life, can be found in many Bible verses. E.g. Deuteronomy 16:14-15 says, *"And thou shalt rejoice in thy feast… therefore thou shalt surely rejoice."* Also, *"My heart shall rejoice in thy salvation."* Psalm 13:5; *"Serve the Lord with gladness: come before his presence with singing."* Psalm 100:2.

The commandment to rejoice (*Simcha shel mitzvah)* accompanied Jews throughout history. They were (and still are) to enjoy each happy event in the Jewish life cycle - from circumcision to *bar mitzvah* to marriage. And above all, there is continuous joy in celebrating the pilgrim festivals and the *Shabbat.*

Since 1989, my husband Wim (William) and I have the privilege to live in Jerusalem, Israel. That is the reason we also were able to celebrate many of the holidays and events described in this book. As a non-Jew who loves Israel and its People, it is wonderful to be able to celebrate the Biblical Feasts and commemorations with the Jewish people. Especially during ceremonies like the swearing in of IDF soldiers, one experiences that the People of Israel are truly one big family - the Apple of God's eye.

I hope this book will help many you to understand and appreciate the Biblical Festivals, Jewish Holidays and Events even more. Learning more about the culture of the Jewish people will (hopefully) result in a deeper love of the Word of God.

Petra van der Zande
Jerusalem, Israel
Sukkot, October 2017

TABLE OF CONTENTS

TABLE OF CONTENT S

TABLE OF CONTENTS

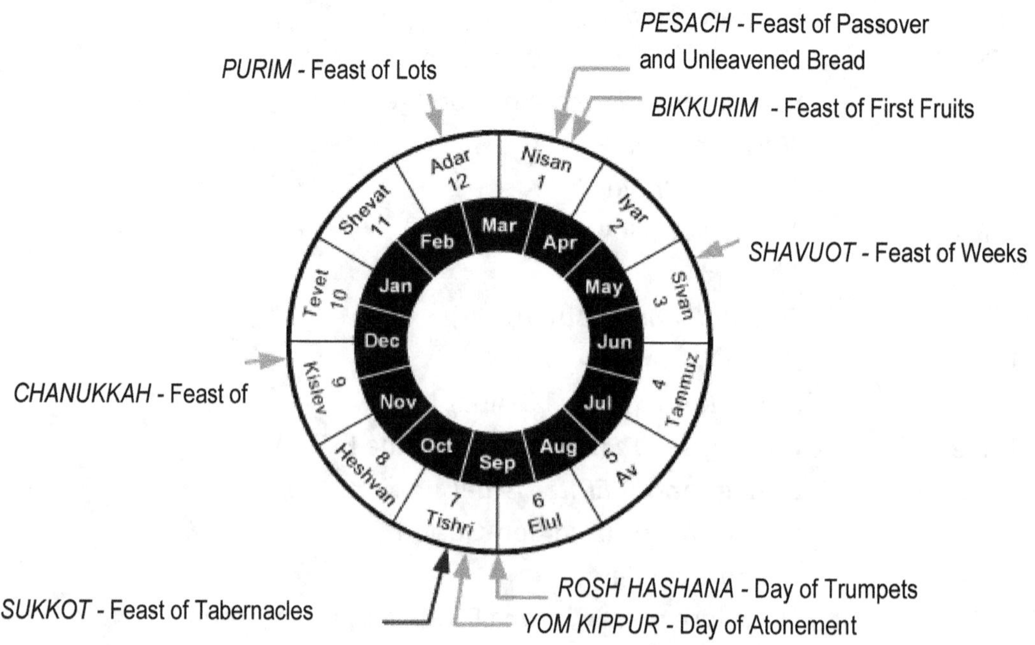

Religious Jewish year: starts on the 1st of the 1st month (Nisan) - *Pesach*
Civil Jewish year: starts on the 1st of the 7th month with Jewish New Year (*Tishri*) - *Rosh Hashana*

Ashkenazim and Sephardim

What is the Difference?

The difference between Ashkenazim and Sephardim is mainly found in their prayer rites. Sephardic prayer customs trace back to Babylonian Jewry, while the Ashkenazi trace their liturgical tradition to the Jews of *Eretz Yisrael.*

The prayer books are ordered in a different way, and there are different cantillation melodies for reading the Pentateuch.

Each community also has unique wedding, circumcision, burial and festival customs and traditions. E.g., during Pesach the Sephardim eat rice, food that is forbidden to the Ashkenazim.

In Israel, both communities have lived side by side for centuries. During the British Mandate period, the chief rabbinate was established with both a Sephardic and Ashkenazi chief rabbi. This continues to this day.

Yona Metzger (Ashkenazi) and
Shlomo Amar (Sefardi)

CHAPTER 1

THE JEWISH CALENDAR

Israel has two calendars - the Western (Gregorian) calendar, and the Jewish religious (Lunar) calendar. Because Jewish holidays follow the Lunar calendar, the Western dates vary each year. A Jewish day begins at sundown, therefore celebrations commence in the evening, and not in the morning.

Even though the year is solar, the Jewish calendar follows lunar months, each with 29 or 30 days. Some scholars believe that lunar months derive from ancient nomadic calendars and solar years are the invention of agricultural societies; the Jewish calendar combines the two.

All the Biblical Feasts (*Pesach, Shavuot and Sukkot)* begin on the full moon, in the middle of the month. Since 12 lunar months do not add up to one complete solar year, additional "leap months" are intercalated into the calendar in seven years out of a 19-year cycle.
The 30-day month is called *maleh* (full) and the 29-day month is called *chaser* (defective).

Gregorian Calendar - Solar year
about 365¼ days
every 4 years a leap day (February 29)

Jewish Calendar - Lunar year
354 days (= 11¼ day less)
every 2 or 3 years a leap month (2nd Adar)

CHAPTER 2

SHABBAT - SABBATH

Shabbat (Yiddish: *shabbes)* is the seventh day of the Jewish week - a day of rest. After six days of creation, God sanctified the *Shabbat*. The word comes from the Hebrew *shavat* (rest, or ceasing from work). It is a holy day (Genesis 2:1-3) and was first commanded after the Exodus from Egypt (Exodus 16:26); it is the fourth of the Ten Commandments (Exodus 20:8-11). In ancient times, desecrating the *Shabbat* was punished by stoning. Only in case of *pikuach nefesh* – when a human life is in danger, the *Shabbat* can (and even has to) be violated. Someone who adheres to the *Shabbat* Laws is called a shomer *Shabbat*.

The *Shabbat* has three purposes:

- To remember – *yizkor* – the redemption from Egyptian slavery
- To commemorate – *shamor* – God's creation of the universe
- It is a foretaste of Messianic times

A typical *Shabbat* begins on Friday afternoon, between 2 and 3 p.m. when observant Jews leave their work or close their shop and head home. Everything is prepared as if a queen or special, beloved guest is expected. The house is cleaned, family members take a shower and put on festive clothes. The table is set with nice tableware, and a festive meal is cooked.

No later than 18 minutes before sunset, the woman of the house makes a blessing over two *Shabbat* candles:
"Blessed are you, Lord, our God, sovereign of the universe, Who has sanctified us with His commandments and commanded us to light the lights of Shabbat. Amen."
The two candles represent the commandment to *zechor* (remember) and *shemor* (to keep) the *Shabbat* holy.

The men walk to the nearby synagogue where they attend a brief service (45 minutes). *Shabbat* services commence on Friday evening with the weekday *Mincha**, followed by *Kabbalat Shabbat* (lit. receiving the Sabbath) and the singing of *Yedid Nefesh.*

Kabbalat Shabbat prayers are composed of six psalms: 95-99 and 29, representing the six week-days.

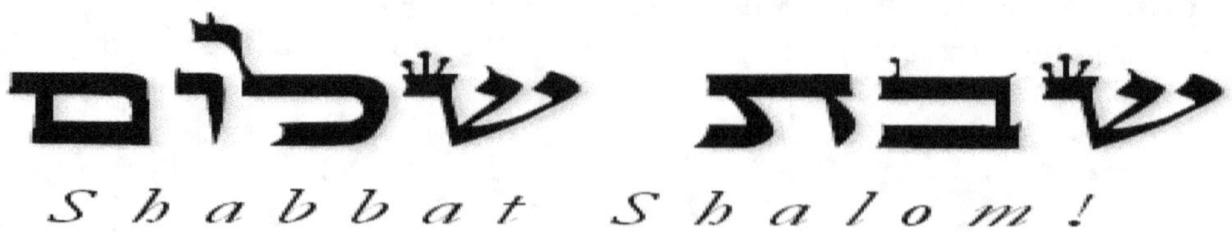

During the singing of the last verse, the entire congregation rises and turns to the open door, to greet the Sabbath Queen as she arrives. *Lecha Dodi,* a liturgical song, is part of the *Kabbalat Shabbat* service on Friday afternoon. *Lecha Dodi* means "come my beloved," and is a request of a mysterious "beloved" that could mean either God or one's friend(s) to join together in welcoming *Shabbat. Likrat kallah* ("to greet the [*Shabbat*] bride").

LECHA DODI

Come, my beloved, to greet the Bride,
Let us welcome in Shabbat !
"Observe" and "Remember" in a
single word;
Our incomparable God made us hear.
Adonai is One, and God's name is One,
Famous, glorious, and praiseworthy.
Let us go out and greet Shabbat,
Because it is the source of blessing.
Honored from the beginning, from
ancient times;
The end of creation, but in thought the
first.
Wake up! Wake up!
For your light has come, rise up and shine!
Awaken! Awaken! Utter a song:
The glory of God is revealed in you!
Enter in peace, crowning of our mastery,
Also in gladness, and in joy,
Amidst the faithful, the holy people,
Enter, Bride. Enter, Bride.

During the singing of the last verse, the entire congregation rises and turns to the open door, to greet "Queen *Shabbat*" as she arrives. The service is concluded by reciting Psalm 92 and 93.

Lecha Dodi was composed in the 16th century by rabbi Shlomo Halevi Alkabetz, a Safed Kabbalist. As was common at the time, the song is also an acrostic - the first letters spell the author's name. Much of the phraseology comes from Isaiah's prophecy of Israel's restoration, and picture Israel as the bride on that great *Shabbat* when Messiah appears.

Before the meal begins, parents bless their children. The father or mother places his or her hands lightly on the child's head, and blesses the boy by saying: *"May God make you like Ephraim and Menashe."*
A girl is blessed with: *"May God make you like Sarah, Rebecca, Rachel and Leah."*
Together, the children are blessed with: *"May God bless you and watch over you. May God shine His face toward you and show you favor. May God be favorably disposed toward you, and may He grant you peace."*

The mother is blessed with Proverbs 31.

The host then takes a cup of wine and recites Kiddush – a prayer over wine, sanctifying the Shabbat:
"Blessed are you, Lord, our God, sovereign of the universe Who creates the fruit of the vine. Amen."

Challot (the Hebrew plural of *challah*) are the braided loaves traditionally eaten on *Shabbat*. Usually there are two challot because on Friday, God gave the wandering Israelites a double portion of manna, so they could rest on the *Shabbat*. Often, the challot are braided, symbolic of the 12 showbreads in the Temple, (one for each tribe) and of the unity of Israel.

The dinner table symbolizes the altar in the Temple. Offerings were salted before being eaten, that is why the bread is sprinkled with salt.

The blessing over the bread:
"Blessed are you LORD, our God, King of the Universe, Who brings forth bread from the earth."
Each person at the table receives a piece of bread, and all eat it together.

Part of the *Oneg* (enjoyment) *Shabbat* is the three festive meals (*shalosh se'udot*). The first is eaten on Friday evening, the second is a *Shabbat* lunch, and the third a light meal, usually dairy, on *Shabbat* afternoon.

After the festive Friday evening dinner, the *birkat ha-mazon* (grace after meals) is recited. In observant households, men study and talk about Torah before going to bed.

Shabbat morning services are usually held from 9 a.m. till noon.

During the morning service, the Torah scroll is taken out of the Ark*, and the weekly portion is read, followed by the *haftarah**. Some communities recite prayers for the government of the country, for peace, and for the State of Israel. Before returning the Torah scroll to the Ark, it is carried through the Synagogue. People touch or kiss the scroll as it passes. In many Orthodox communities, the rabbi (or a learned member of the congregation) delivers a sermon, usually on the topic of the Torah reading.

In Orthodox families, the second meal often is a slow-cooked stew – cholent. Sephardic Jews call it *chamim.* This is followed by more Torah study. In the afternoon, many families, dressed in their *Shabbat* finery, go out for a walk, read or take a nap.

Shabbat ends at nightfall, when three stars are visible – about 40 minutes after sunset.

Now is the time for the *Havdalah** (separation, division) ceremony that ushers in the new week. A special braided *Havdalah* candle (with several wicks) is lit and a prayer recited.

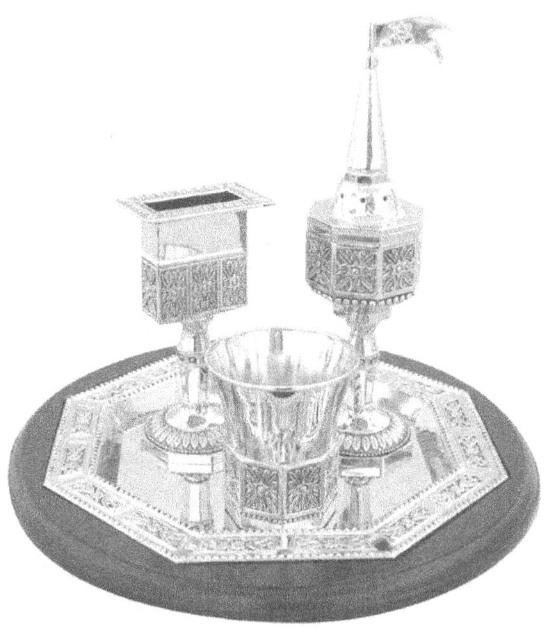

The guests at the table stare at their fingernails which (are supposed to) reflect the light of the candle.

Spices, often stored in a decorative container, are passed around to smell the fragrance. *Havdalah* requires the use of all five senses – taste the wine, smell the spices, see the candle's flame and feel its heat and hear the blessings over the symbols. It marks the separation between the sacred *Shabbat* and the secular new week which now has begun.
Everyone wishes each other a, *"Shavua tov!"* - "a good week!"

The beautiful poem *Yedid Nefesh* is commonly attributed to the sixteenth century kabbalist, Rabbi Elazar ben Moshe Azikri (1533-1600). Some sing it between Friday afternoon prayer and the beginning of *Kabbalat Shabbat*. Many Jewish families also sing this song during the third (and last) *Shabbat*'s meal before nightfall, and the beginning of a new day and week, Sunday.

YEDID NEFESH

Beloved of the soul, Compassionate Father,
draw Your servant to Your will.
Then Your servant will hurry like a gazelle
to bow before Your majesty.
To him Your friendship will be sweeter
than the dripping of the honeycomb
and all taste.

Majestic, beautiful, radiance of the universe
my soul is sick for your love.
Please O G-d, heal her now by showing
her the pleasantness of Your radiance.
Then she will be strengthened and healed
and eternal gladness will be hers.

All worthy One - may Your mercy be aroused
and please take pity on the son of Your beloved, because it is so very long
that I have yearned intensely
to see the splendor of Your strength,
only these my heart desired,
so please take pity and do not conceal Yourself.

Please be revealed and spread upon me, my Beloved,
the shelter of Your peace
that we may rejoice and be glad with You.
Hasten, beloved, for the time has come,
and show us grace as in days of old.

A SHABBAT JOURNEY

"A Sabbath day's journey" isn't a phrase used by Jews, but Christian in origin.

In ancient times, rabbis based the rules on how far one was allowed to travel from the city boundaries on Joshua 3:4-5.

"Yet there shall be a space between you and it, about two thousand cubits by measure: come not near unto it, that ye may know the way by which ye must go: for ye have not passed this way heretofore."

The rabbis concluded that "place" meant city, and therefore it was acceptable to travel 2,000 cubits outside his city limits on the *Shabbat*. The Pharisees had a different interpretation, and allowed a journey of 4,000 cubits (about 6,000 feet) - a little over a mile. In New Testament times they theorized that if a person was to travel 4,000 cubits on the *Shabbat,* then he would also need to return and thus they allowed 8,000 cubits as the standard.

(Negative) *Mitzvah** #321 sets the maximum walking range from one's city to 2,000 cubits (3,049.5 feet, 0.596 miles (960 meters). [However, this measurement starts 70 2/3 cubits (112.24 ft.) from the city limits.] Practically speaking, this means that one may not walk a straight line more than .598 miles (3161.74 ft.) in any direction in the wilds outside the city limits.

THE *SHABBOS GOY*

A *Shabbos goy* (Yiddish) or in Hebrew, *goy shel Shabbat* is a non-Jew who performs certain types of work for a Jew on the *Shabbat* which according to Jewish Law (*Halacha**) they are is forbidden to perform. *"Goy"* in Biblical Hebrew literally means "a nation", but is mainly used to typify a "non-Jew".

Because a Jew has to respect a non-Jew's right to rest on the Shabbat, they may not explicitly ask them to perform a service which is prohibited to the Jewish people.

However, as a non-Jew is not expected to keep the *Shabbat* like a Jew, they can perform tasks of their own free will. It often happens that a Jew hints to a non-Jew that he wants him to perform a certain service without explicitly asking him. Such cases are considered legitimate in most Jewish communities.

Before the 20th century, *Shabbos goys* most commonly extinguished the lighted candles or lamps on Friday night, and made a fire in the oven or stove on *Shabbat* mornings during cold weather. A *Shabbat goyah* usually was a poor woman who was paid with a piece of *Challah* or 10 cents.

Even today, in many Jewish communities it is considered legitimate to hire a non-Jewish worker to perform certain services on the *Shabbat*, providing that the non-Jew is paid in advance, so that the payment seems like a kind of gift rather than a salary.

A *shabbat (or Shabbes) goy* is not needed where life is at stake (*pikuach nefesh*). Religious Jewish physicians also work on the *Shabbat*, but often leave the paperwork to the *Shabbes Goy.*

Some ultra-orthodox households, synagogues and neighborhoods have their 'own' *Shabbos goy*.

Abu Ali, a modern-day *Shabbos goy* in Jerusalem

From sundown Friday to sundown Saturday, Abu Ali (his nickname) serves Jerusalem's ultra-Orthodox Jewish community as a *Shabbos goy*.

The 55-year-old Muslim turns on air conditioners when it's hot, and when someone accidentally left on his lights, he turns them off. When a fuse blows, he comes to the house to replace them. Each Shabbat, he has to drive one or more women to the hospital to give birth.

Abu Ali's Muslim friends and neighbors do not know what kind of work he does on *Shabbat*. He is an atypical Muslim serving Orthodox Jews in a city where the two communities more often collide than connect. On *Shabbat*, he feels like a king in the ultra-Orthodox community. Everyone knows him. And needs him. After the day of rest, however, he reverts to be the 'unknown' Muslim. He takes it all in stride.

In the early days of his 'career' as a *Shabbos goy*, Abu Ali helped out in the emergency room of a nearby hospital. When that closed, he moved down the street to the nearby ultra-orthodox neighborhood. When his duties as a *Shabbes goy* begin, he makes himself comfortable in his 'own' plastic shed with plastic chair and a small refrigerator filled with soda. Taped to the shed door, in big black Hebrew letters on fluorescent-yellow paper it says: *Shabbos Goy*.

Orthodox Jews are not allowed to ask for help, so the community uses their special code with Abu Ali. When they come to tell him that, "It is hot today, Abu Ali," he knows they want him to turn the air conditioner on. "It is dark," means he has to turn a light on, or replace a fuse.

Abu Ali doesn't work for free - he charges about $10 per visit and rushing a pregnant woman to the hospital costs about $30. Because ultra-orthodox families are not supposed to pay their *Shabbos Goy* for his services, people put the money in a box outside the neighborhood synagogue. After the Shabbat, of course.

Adapted from an article in The Seattle Times Company , 2008, by Dion Nissenbaum.

A Synagogue is a Jewish or Samaritan house of prayer.

Greek: *synagogē* (assembly)
Septuagint: *kahal* (assembly)
Modern Hebrew: *bayt knesset* (house of assembly) or *beyt t'fila* (house of prayer)
Yiddish: *shul* (from German schule - school)
Ladino: *esnoga*
Persian and Karaite Jews: *kenesa* (Aramaic)
Arabic: *knis*
Reform and Conservative Jews: temple

THE SYNAGOGUE

"…to love the Lord your God, and to serve him with all your heart and with all your soul."
Deuteronomy 11:13

"What service is performed with the heart?" the Talmud asks. "This is prayer."
Prayers are therefore referred to as *Avodah sheba-Lev* (service that is in the heart).

Tefilláh (plural *tefillos or tefillót*); Yiddish: *davnen** (to pray) are recitations which can be found in the siddur, the traditional Jewish prayer book.

Various prayers are said upon arising and when the *tallit katan** (a garment with *tzitzit**) is donned. Blessings accompany the donning of the *tallit** (large prayer shawl) before or during the prayer service in synagogue, and the *tefillin** (phylacteries).

Most synagogues have a *Hechal**, a large hall for prayer (the main sanctuary).

SAYINGS ABOUT PRAYER

◊ When praying, cast down your eyes and lift up your hearts.
◊ Let those who are ignorant of Hebrew learn the prayers in their own daily languages, since prayer must be understood.
◊ If the heart does not know what the lips utter, it is no prayer.
◊ A poor man's prayer breaks through every barrier and storms its way into the presence of the Almighty.
◊ The gates of prayer are never closed.
◊ Prayer is conversation with God.

Readings from the Torah* (five books of Moses) and the *Nevi'im* * (Prophets) form part of the prayer services.

Communal prayer with a *minyan* * is preferable as it permits the inclusion of prayers that otherwise must be omitted when praying individually .

Daily Prayer Services

◊   *Shacharit or Shaharit* (from the Hebrew *shachar or shahar* -morning light)
◊   *Mincha or Minha* (afternoon prayers named for the flour offering that accompanied sacrifices at the Temple in Jerusalem.) Time: From half an hour after (halachic) noontime until 2.5 hours before nightfall). One is expected to complete the prayers before sunset.
◊   *Ma'ariv/Arvit* (evening prayers) Time: nightfall. On a working day, the afternoon and evening prayers are recited back-to-back to save people having to come to synagogue twice.

Additional Prayers
◊   *Musaf* (additional) recited by Orthodox and Conservative congregations on *Shabbat*, major Jewish holidays (including *Chol HaMoed* * and *Rosh Chodesh* *)
◊   *Ne'ilah* (closing) is a fifth prayer service which is recited only on *Yom Kippur*, the Day of Atonement.

There are usually also smaller rooms for study, sometimes a social hall for occasions and offices for bookkeeping. Some synagogues have a separate room for a *bayit midrash* * (House of Torah Study).

Communal Jewish worship can be carried out wherever a *minyan* * (ten Jewish men) assemble. Worship can also be carried out alone or with fewer than ten people assembled together.

Orthodox synagogues feature a *mechitzah* * (partition) dividing the men's and women's seating areas, or a separate women's section located on a balcony.

Over the last two thousand years, variations have emerged among the traditional liturgical customs of different Jewish communities, such as Ashkenazi, Sephardic, Yemenite, Chassidic and others. Most of the Jewish liturgy is sung or chanted with traditional melodies or trope.

A professional or lay *chazzan* * (cantor) often leads the congregation in prayer, especially on *Shabbat* or holidays.

According to the Talmud, the Biblical commandment to pray is to recall the daily sacrifices at the Temple in Jerusalem.
The Patriarch Abraham instituted the morning prayer, Isaac the afternoon prayer, and Jacob the evening prayer.

From the Bible we know that King David and the prophet Daniel prayed three times a day.

> *... Evening, and morning, and at noon, will I pray, and cry aloud: and he shall hear my voice.* **Psalm 55:17**
>
> *... his windows being open in his chamber toward Jerusalem, he kneeled upon his knees three times a day, and prayed, and gave thanks before his God, as he did aforetime.* **Daniel 6:10**

*Halacha** (Jewish law) requires Jewish men to pray three times daily; four times on the Shabbat and most Jewish holidays; five times on *Yom Kippur*.
Orthodox Jewish women are required to pray at least once daily, with no specific time requirement.
Because of the endless cycle of pregnancy, birthing and nursing (often from an early age), women are exempted from almost all time-specific positive *mitzvot** (commandments).

Even though all individual prayers and the majority of communal prayers may be said in any language that the person understands, most Ashkenazi Orthodox synagogues use Hebrew prayers. Sephardic communities may use Ladino or Portuguese for many prayers, while Conservative and Reform synagogues tend to use the local language.

Judaism originally only counted men in the minyan for formal prayer. Today, Conservative congregations count women in the minyan and even have female rabbis and cantors.

In most synagogues, it is considered a sign of respect for Jewish (and non-Jewish) male attendees to wear a head covering, either a dress hat or a *kippah** (skull cap or yarmulke). Married women cover their hair with a wig, scarf, hat or a combination of them.

A *tallit* (prayer shawl) is traditionally worn during all morning services, during *Aliyah** to the Torah, as well as the *Kol Nidre** service of *Yom Kippur*.
During afternoon and evening services only the *chazzan* wears a *tallit*.

Tefillin (phylacteries) are worn by orthodox men only during weekday morning prayers. Conservative synagogues allow women to don tefillin.

Some Synagogue Prayers

- *Birkot ha-shachar* (morning blessings)
- *Pesukei D'Zimrah* (verses of praise: Psalms 100 and 145–150)
- *Barechu* (formal public call to prayer; incl. recitation of the *Shema*)
- *Amidah or Shemoneh Esreh* (a series of 19 blessings)
- *Tachanun* (supplications)
- *Shema Yisrael* (Hear O Israel from Deuteronomy 6:4 v.v.)
- Priestly Blessing (Numbers 6:24-26)
- *Aleinu*
- *Kaddish* (mourner's prayer)
- *Uva letzion* (and [a redeemer] shall come to Zion). Closing prayer before which one should not leave the synagogue.

Shemoneh Esreh (eighteen/ now nineteen blessings), also called the *Amidah* (standing prayer), is traditionally ascribed to the Great Assembly in the time of Ezra. The eighteen prayers of the weekday Amidah became standardized near the end of the Second Temple period. During the Middle Ages the texts of the prayers were set in the form in which they are still used today.

AVINU MALKENU ("Our Father, our King")

These are the opening words and refrain of the most ancient Jewish litany. Ashkenazim recite this prayer after the morning and afternoon service (*Amidah),* during penitential and fast days, especially on *Yom Kippur*, but never on *Tisha beAv.*

"Our Father, our King
Be compassionate to us
and answer us,
for we have no deeds.
Grant us charity and benevolence
and redeem us."

Haftarah*
This is a text selected from the books of *Nevi'im** that is read publicly in the synagogue after the reading of the Torah on each *Shabbat* as well as on Jewish festivals and fast days.

Ketuvim*
Poetic Books: Psalms, Proverbs, Job
Five *Megillot* (scrolls): Song of Songs, Ruth, Lamentations, Ecclesiastes, Esther
Other: Daniel, Ezra - Nehemiah, Chronicles

Nevi'im
Nevi'im (Prophets) is the second of the three major sections in the Hebrew Bible, the Tanach. It falls between the Torah (teachings) and *Ketuvim* (writings). Prophets is traditionally divided into two parts: Earlier Prophets or *Nevi'im Rishonim* which contains the narrative books of Joshua through Kings. Latter Prophets (*Nevi'im Aharonim*) mostly contains prophecies in the form of biblical poetry

Nevi'im Rishonim: Joshua, Judges, Samuel, Kings, Isaiah, Jeremiah, Ezekiel
Nevi'im Aharonim: Hosea, Joel, Amos, Jonah, Obadiah, Micha, Nahum, Habakkuk, Zephaniah, Haggai, Zechariah, Malachi

ADON OLAM (Lord of the Universe)

This is the translation of a popular liturgical hymn which is sung during synagogue services.

"Reigned the Universe's Master,
Ere were earthy things begun;
When His mandate all created,
Ruler was the name He won.
And alone He'll rule tremendous
When all things are past and gone,
He no equal has, nor consort,
He, the singular and lone,
Has no end and no beginning;

His the scepter, might and throne.
He's my God and living Saviour,
Rock to Whom I in need run;
He's my banner and my refuge,
Fount of weal when call'd upon.
In His hand I place my spirit,
At nightfall and at rise of sun,
And therewith my body also;
God's my God - I fear no-one."

TALLIT - PRAYER SHAWL

> **"Thou shalt make thee fringes upon the four quarters of thy vesture, wherewith thou coverest thyself."**
> **Deuteronomy 22:12**

A *tallit* is a Jewish prayer shawl, worn over the outer clothes during morning prayers. Attached to its four corners are *tzitzit**, special twined and knotted fringes.

Tallit is an Aramaic word from the root "*tll*", which means cover, cloak or sheet. From Talmudic times onwards, the word referred to the prayer shawl.

A traditional *tallit* is made of wool, but can be made of any material, except for a mixture of wool and linen. Often, it is given to a son for his *Bar Mitzvah* or to a groom as part of the dowry.

The use of the *tallit* goes back to around 1800 BCE, but the design was different than that known today.

"Speak unto the children of Israel, and bid them that they make them fringes in the borders of their garments throughout their generations, and that they put upon the fringe of the borders a ribband of blue (techelet)..." Numbers 15:38

*Techelet i*s color dye which the Jews were commanded to use for the *tzitzit.*
Over time, the source of the dye was lost and since then, Jews have worn plain white *tzitzyot* without any dyes. The rediscovery of the snail who produces the techelet is seen as a sign of the soon-coming of Messiah!

The purpose of wearing tzitzit is to remind Jews of their religious obligations, and to remember the Exodus from Egypt (See Numbers 15:40).

Observant Jews do this by wearing a *tallit katan* (small *tallit*). The fringed, poncho-like garment is usually worn under their clothing. It has a hole for the head and tzitzit attached to its four corners. A *tallit katan* is often made of wool or cotton.

The prayer shawl, the *tallit gadol,* is worn over the shoulder by all male participants during the morning prayer services in synagogue.
Today, some *tallitot* are made of polyester and cotton. They can be of any color but are usually white with black, blue or white stripes along the edge.

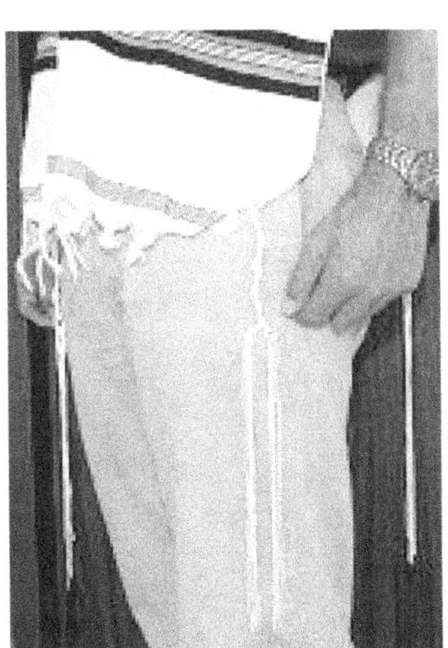

While reciting the *Shema*, it is customary to kiss the *tzitzit* each time the word is mentioned.

TEFILLIN - Phylacteries

Tefillin (Phylacteries) are two small quadrangular black leather boxes with the letter *Shin*, containing four biblical passages. These are worn by male Jews from the age of 13.

Strapped on the left arm and on the head, *Tefillin* are used during weekday morning services in the synagogue. The head strap is tied with a knot in the shape of a *dalet*, while the arm knot is in the shape of a *yud*. Together with the shin on the box, this makes *shin - dalet- yud (Shaddai)* one of the names of God.

The commandment to don tefillin can be found in Exodus 13:1-10; 11-16 and Deuteronomy 6:4-9; 13-21.

Donning tefillin reminds a Jewish man that he is bound up in service to God, with heart, mind and might.

HAIR COVERING AND DRESS CODE

The Bible presents hair as an ornament, enhancing the appearance of a woman. In Biblical times, a betrothed woman had to cover her hair and face with a veil. Cutting a woman's hair was a way to make her unattractive. Deuteronomy 21:12 mentions the laws of the captive woman. Some scholars suggest that cutting the woman's hair made her less attractive to her captor, perhaps even with the intent that by the end of the month his ardor would cool and he would let her go, instead of claiming her as his wife.

Chatam Sofer (1762-1839), a dominant rabbinical scholar and traditionalist, instigated the Jewish law which required a woman to cut her hair after she wed. This practice became prevalent in central Europe and especially Hungary. Although many rabbis were opposed, this ritual took hold in a number of communities.

Covering the Woman's Hair

In post-biblical Judaism, covering of the hair signaled a transition in the female life cycle, symbolizing the departure from maidenhood into womanhood. The woman became inaccessible and unavailable to all but her husband. The veil had to be worn whenever she was in mixed company or went out in public. According to the Mishnah, a woman going about with uncovered hair represented unacceptable conduct.

By the time of the Middle Ages, the religious obligation of covering the hair was firmly entrenched amongst women of all faiths: Jewish, Christian and Muslim.

From Veil to Wig

In 16th century France it became fashionable to wear wigs, which also took hold amongst Jewish women. At first denounced by rabbinic authorities, most eventually accepted the trend, which led to controversy in the more pious Jewish communities.

Some women believed that the wig itself was enough, while others wore a wig with an additional head covering.

On her wedding day, a woman enters into a unique relationship with her husband. Judaism views a woman's hair as a sensual and private part of her appearance. By covering her hair, the woman expresses her exclusive devotion, love for, and unique connection to her husband.

In Biblical times, when a woman was accused by her husband of adultery, she had to appear before the priest. Part of the humiliation that preceded the ceremony was the public uncovering or unbraiding of the woman's hair (Numbers 5:18). From this, the Talmud concludes that under normal circumstances, hair covering is a biblical requirement for women.

A religious married woman is expected to cover her hair, even in a semi-public place where no men are found. Many religious women find meaning in the value of hair covering. To them, it is an essential and distinctive expression of their religious belief.

Different types of hair coverings
◊   *sheitel* (wig)
◊   snood
◊   *mitpachat* (Hebrew: scarf) or *tichel*
     (Yiddish)
◊   hat or beret

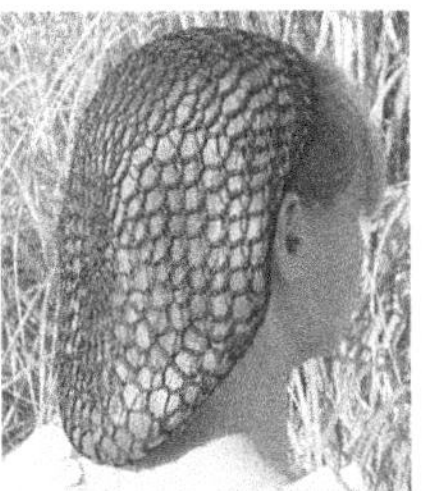

Sheitel or sheytl (Yiddish- probably derived from German *Scheitel*); Dutch: *schedel* (skull); Hebrew: *pei'ah.*

Orthodox Jewish married women are required by Jewish Law to cover their hair. This practice is part of the modesty-related dress standard called *Tzeniut**.
Some Haredi (Ultra-orthodox) women cover their hair with an wig and an additional hat or beret.

Traditional *sheitels* are secured by elastic caps and are often designed with heavy bangs to obscure the hairline of their wearers. Designed lace-front wigs with realistic hairlines are becoming more popular now.
The wig orthodox women wear is *kosher**, one that has a certificate stating that it was not made with hair originating from rituals deemed to be idolatrous. (Most of the hair comes from Indian Hindu temples.)
A style of half wig known as a "fall" has be-come increasingly common in many segments of Modern and Haredi Orthodox communities. It is usually worn with either a hat or head-band.

In order not to show their own hair, some women shave it off or cut it really short. Most Chassidic sects forbid women to wear a *sheitel,* as it may give the impression that the wearer's head is uncovered. Women belonging to the Toldos (Toldot) Aharon often shave their heads bald and cover them with a kerchief. The strongly anti-Zionist Chassidic movement is headquartered in Jerusalem's Meah Shearim

neighborhood.
Most unmarried Haredi girls wear their hair in a simple ponytail, while those of the Toldot Aharon have their hair in two braids.

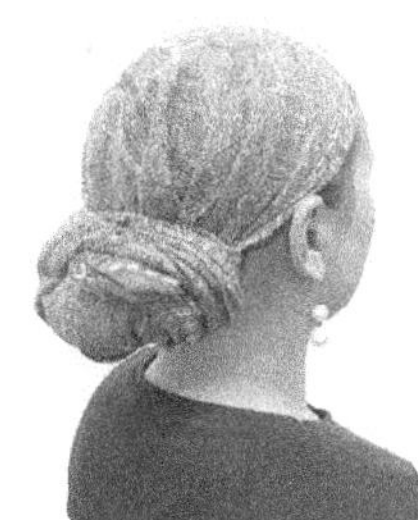

Sephardic married women and those who are National Religious do not wear wigs. According to their rabbis, these head coverings are insufficiently modest - a hat or *tichel (mitpachat)* is more suitable.
Tichels can range from a simple, plain color cotton square with a simple tie in the back to an elaborate *mitpachat* with multiple fabrics. These are both fashionable and modest.

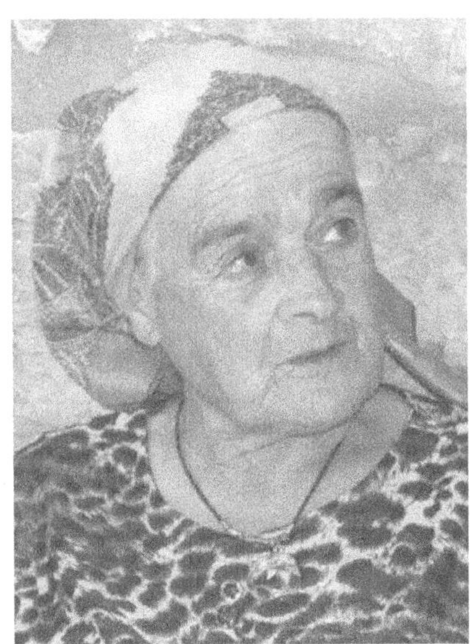

Orthodox Jewish Dress Code

Orthodox Judaism requires both men and women to substantially cover their bodies, i.e. modest clothing.

MEN:

In Haredi (ultra-Orthodox) communities, men generally wear long trousers and long-sleeved shirts. While Modern Orthodox men sometimes wear shorts and short-sleeved shirts, Haredi men will never do such a thing. Sandals without socks (except in synagogue), are usually accepted in Modern Orthodox and Israeli Religious Zionist Communities for daily dress. Haredi Ashkenazi practice discourages sandals without socks. Haredi Sephardic communities tend to accept sandals outside and sometimes even in synagogue.

Foto: Mercy Gaynoor

WOMEN:

Orthodox women wear long sleeved blouses (often with an additional loose vest over it), and skirts covering the knees. Haredi women avoid skirts with slits and eye-catching colors, like bright red. Most wear closed-toe shoes and stockings - the approved thickness depends on the community.

Modern Orthodox women generally wear shirts or blouses covering the collarbone and 3/4 sleeves; skirts mostly over the knees or long. Some women do wear trousers.

Many religious Jews believe that the way one dresses for synagogue and in public should be comparable to the clothes one wears when meeting royalty or government officials.

Code of Behavior

In Orthodox Judaism, unrelated men and women are not allowed to touch each other. (A quick handshake at a business meeting is sometimes allowed.) Refraining from touching the opposite sex is called *shemirat negiah**. Parents, children, grandparents and grandchildren do not fall under this category; neither does one's spouse, unless she is *niddah** (ritually impure during and after menstruation). Many observant married couples will not touch one another in public.

Unrelated orthodox men and women are not allowed to enter into a secluded situation (*yichud**) in a room or in an area that is private and where no one else is expected to enter. This is to prevent possible unlawful sexual relations. For this reason people leave the door ajar when conducting a meeting, or make sure there are more people in the room. Originally, this prohibition applied only to married women secluded with men other than their husbands.

After King David's son Amnon raped Absalom's sister Tamar, the yichud prohibition was extended to include single women as well.

CHAPTER 3

ROSH CHODESH

"Also in the day of your gladness, and in your solemn days, and in the beginnings of your months, ye shall blow with the trumpets over your burnt offerings, and over the sacrifices of your peace offerings; that they may be to you for a memorial before your God: I am the Lord your God." **Numbers 10:10**

Rosh Chodesh (lit. "head of the month") is the name for the first day of every month in the Hebrew calendar, marked by the day and hour that the moon's new crescent is observed. It is considered a minor holiday, akin to *Chol Hamo'ed**, the intermediate days of *Pesach and Sukkot.*

The Hebrew calendar was established while the Israelites were still in Egypt: *"And the Lord spake unto Moses and Aaron in the land of Egypt saying, This month shall be unto you the beginning of months: it shall be the first month of the year to you."* Exodus 12:1-2

Both new and full moon are also mentioned in Psalm 81:3.

In ancient times, a new month was determined by observers watching the sky at night for any sign of the moon. The sighting of the first sliver of moon was immediately reported to the Sanhedrin. (The highest court of justice and the supreme council in ancient Jerusalem.) The Jewish leaders asked where in the sky the moon appeared, and in which direction it was pointing. Only if two independent, reliable eye-witnesses confirmed that the new moon had appeared and described it consistently, the Sanhedrin would declare the new month.

Messengers went out to tell people the month had begun. Fires were lit on the hilltops to announce the new month to neighboring communities who, in turn, passed the message along.

Rosh Chodesh became a significant festival day. It was announced with the blowing of the shofar*, commemorated with solemn convocations, family festivities and special sacrifices. In ancient times the yearly festivals and Feasts were dependent on these declarations.
After the destruction of the Temple, when sacrifices were no longer available, the significance of *Rosh Chodesh* diminished.

The present Jewish calendar was introduced in the time of Hillel II (358/9 CE). Astronomical calculations replaced the practice of calling witnesses before the Sanhedrin. On the basis of scientific calculations it now was possible to calculate the Jewish calendar well into the future.

Today, *Rosh Chodesh* is publicly announced on the *Shabbat* before it occurs, except in the month of *Rosh Hashanah* (the Jewish New Year).
Because there is a special benediction recited during the Torah Service, this day is called the *Shabbat Mevarechim* (the Sabbath of Blessing).

During the evening service of *Rosh Chodesh* a prayer is added for the restoration of the Temple. The next morning, the prayer is recited again, together with all or part of the Hallel (Psalms 113-118). Numbers 28:1-15 is also read. The *Musaf* is an additional prayer service which commemorates the original sacrifices in the Temple. After the service, many recite Psalm 104.

It is customary to eat a special meal in honor of *Rosh Chodesh.*
The *Kiddush Levanah** (sanctification of the moon) is typically recited on the first Saturday night after *Rosh Chodesh.*

According to the Talmud, women are exempt from work on *Rosh Chodesh.* Rashi (1040-1105 AD), the famous Jewish scholar, described the activities they were allowed to refrain from:

spinning, weaving, and sewing. This was the type of work women did when the *Mishkan* (Tabernacle) was prepared.

Rosh Chodesh has long been recognized as a women's holiday. Because of the day's special character, it is customary to wear new clothing on this day.

Religious women celebrating *Rosh Chodesh* at Tel Shiloh, the place where the Tabernacle once stood.

CHAPTER FOUR

PESACH - PASSOVER

Pesach, Passover, the first of the three Jewish Pilgrim's festivals, is always celebrated on the 14th day of the Hebrew month of Nisan. This day marks the beginning of the Biblical New Year. The date also determined the length of a king's reign.

Passover commemorates the Exodus from Egypt when God delivered the Israelites from bondage.

The Shabbat before Passover is called the *Shabbat haGadol** because it marks the beginning of the redemption.

Today, observant Jews spend the weeks before Passover in a flurry of thorough housecleaning to remove all morsels of *chametz** from every part of the home. This 'spring-cleaning' ritual has been copied by many non-Jews as well.

Chametz (leavening) is made from one of five types of grains which combined with water are left to stand for more than eighteen minutes. During Passover, it is forbidden to eat, keep or own olive-sized or larger quantities of *chametz*.

Most orthodox Jews go even further - even the cracks of kitchen counters are thoroughly scrubbed to remove any traces of flour and yeast, however small. Any item or implement that has handled *chametz* is generally put away and not used during Passover.

It is possible to sell chametz to a non-Jew (who is not obligated to observe the commandments) in exchange for a symbolic fee (e.g. $1.00). Generally, people 'sell' their *chametz* to a rabbi who in turn acts as an agent and sells it to a non-Jew. The rabbi re-purchases the goods for less than they were sold at the end of the holiday.

Some people create a special *chametz* cupboard where they store their items until after the holiday. Supermarket shelves containing products that are not *kosher lePesach* (kosher for Passover) are covered with plastic sheets.

Most observant families have special sets of serving dishes, glassware and silverware (and in some cases, even separate dishwashers and sinks) which have never come into contact with *chametz.* These are only used during Passover. Certain utensils, like flatware and metal pots and pans can be made '*kosher* for Passover' use through a process known as "kashering." In religious neighborhoods the *kashering* service is offered for a small amount of money.

The search for remaining leaven takes place on the evening before Passover. After a special blessing, one or more members of the household go from room to room to check that no crumbs remain in any corner.

The search is conducted by candlelight (illuminating corners without casting shadows), a feather (to get crumbs out of their hiding places), and a wooden spoon (to collect the crumbs). These are to be burned the next day with the rest of the *chametz*. It is customary to hide ten morsels of bread smaller than the size of an olive to ensure that some *chametz* will be found.

On the morning of the 14th of Nisan, all leavened products that were still in the house are burned. In order to ensure a safe burning of the *chametz,* municipalities place special incinerators on the street corners.

That same morning, firstborn sons are commanded to observe the Fast of the Firstborn which commemorates the salvation of the Hebrew firstborns. According to Exodus 12:29, God struck all Egyptian firstborns while the Israelites were not affected.

It is customary for synagogues to conduct a *siyum** (ceremony marking the completion of a section of Torah learning) right after morning prayers.

The festive meal that follows cancels the firstborn's obligation to fast.

Pesach is also called *Chag haMatsot*, referring to the flat, unleavened "bread". The Israelites had to leave in such a hurry that there was no time for the bread to rise. God told the Israelites to eat unleavened bread for seven days.

During the 40 years in the desert there was only manna. Upon entering the Promised Land, the Jewish people were able to bake *matzot* from the local wheat and barley in order to celebrate a true *Pesach.*

Korban Pesach is the lamb that was killed at the Tabernacle and Temple, roasted and eaten during the holiday.
The Prophet Samuel revived the national religious festival and under King Solomon the Feast took new splendor with the building of the First Temple. After his death, idolatry and paganism caused the *Pesach* celebrations to decline. Godly kings like Hezekiah and Josiah reinstated the Festival. After the destruction of the First Temple the *Korban Pesach* could no longer be sacrificed and was replaced by prayers, eating matza and bitter herbs. When the Second Temple was built, the *Korban Pesach* again was reinstated, until the destruction of the Temple in 70 A.D.

Worldwide, more than 80% of the Jewish people attend a Seder on the eve of the holiday.

Seder means order and refers to the commemoration of the Exodus from Egypt by eating special types of food, reading the Biblical story and singing specific songs.
Some of today's practices were already followed before the destruction of the second Temple in the homes of Jews who couldn't go on pilgrimage to Jerusalem.

The *Pesach Haggadah* contains the text and order of the Seder meal, which can take many hours to complete.

Early on the Monday and Thursday morning of the intermediary days, the priestly blessing takes place at the Western Wall in Jerusalem's Old City.
Cohanim (whose names indicate they are of the priestly line of Aaron) give the Aharonic blessing from Numbers 6:24-26, while covered with their *talllits* (prayer shawls).

The priestly blessing or priestly benediction, *birkat cohanim,* is also known as *nesiat kapayim* (raising of the hands), or *dukhanen* (from the Yiddish word *dukhan* - platform - because the blessing used to be given from a raised rostrum).

In Israel, the *Pesach* holiday is observed for seven days; in the Diaspora, for eight days. The first and last days are major holidays, on which working is prohibited (like a *Shabbat)*. During *Chol Hamoed* (intermediate days), people are allowed to work.

The Samaritans living on Mount Gerazim, near Shechem (Nablus) and the Ethiopian Falashas are the only group of people still performing Paschal sacrifices during *Pesach*.

Pesach Gerazim, 1934

Pesach is a real family holiday that everyone enjoys. During this time, many cars begin to display a national flag.

ISRU CHAG

*Isru Chag** literally means "bind the festival offering" or "the day after the Feast".
During Temple times, pilgrims who had come to Jerusalem on pilgrimage, began their long journey home on this day. Today, *isru chag,* (the extra holiday after the three Pilgrim Festivals), is observed as a minor holiday.

A tree may be alone in the field,
A man alone in the world,
But no Jew is alone
on his holy days.

Abba Kovner

BIRKAT COHANIM – PRIESTLY BLESSING

"Speak unto Aaron and unto his sons, saying, On this wise ye shall bless the children of Israel, saying unto them, The Lord bless thee, and keep thee: The Lord make his face shine upon thee, and be gracious unto thee: The Lord lift up his countenance upon thee, and give thee peace. And they shall put my name upon the children of Israel, and I will bless them."
Numbers 6:23-27

Birkat Cohanim is the Hebrew name for the "blessing of the Priests". (Cohen = priest). In the time Temple era, the Priests recited this blessing every day.

Today there are synagogues that perform this rite every morning, others only on Shabbat. In the Diaspora the ceremony usually takes place only on Jewish holidays, when most of the congregation is together.

During the blessing, the hands of the Cohanim are spread out over the congregation with the fingers held in such a way they form the Hebrew letter Shin. This symbolizes the light of the *Shekhina* - Presence of God.

In many congregations the men spread their *tallitot* (prayer shawls) over their heads and don't look at the Cohanim, so as not to get distracted. During the Pilgrim Festivals a special ceremony takes place at the Western Wall (Kotel).

It is customary to have the priestly hand gesture engraved on tombstones of Cohanim.
The words of the priestly blessing, etched on silver scrolls, were found by archeologists in tombs dating from the seventh century BC.

Mr. Spock, from the Star Trek television series, used the single handed version of the priestly blessing as the "Live long and prosper" greeting.

CHAPTER FIVE

PRAYING FOR DEW

> *"Dew, precious dew… fall upon the land. From heaven's treasury be this recorded…"* (Ashkenazi prayer)

At the end of the *Pesach* holiday, prayers for dew are inserted into the synagogue services. Passover occurs at the end of the rainy season and heralds the beginning of summer. The first rain (Yoreh) can only be expected in October or November. In Israel, dew was (and still is) of utmost importance during the hot, dry summer months.

Life-giving dew continues to be seen as a blessing from heaven. In many congregations it is customary for the cantor to wear a white garment, *kittel,* as he does on the High Holidays, when reciting the prayers for dew, so as to arouse the Divine mercy which God metes out on Passover for the crops.

Between *Pesach and Shavuot*, the seven species (date, olive, fig, grape, barley wheat and pomegranate) are in various stages of maturing. Each type of fruit needs different climatic situations to ensure an abundant harvest. At this time of the year, the weather is often unstable - sudden heat-waves can be followed by cold spells. Therefore, the outcome of the season's crop is never sure.

During Temple times, farmers brought *Bikkurim* (first fruits) from the seven species. They had to depend on the One true God, as opposed to the heathen people who believed pagan gods controlled the climate.

PREPARING FOR MINOUNA

On the evening the *Pesach* holiday ends, Moroccan Jews begin to celebrate their Mimouna Festival.

CHAPTER SIX

MIMOUNA FESTIVAL

This traditionally North African Jewish celebration marks the start of spring and the return to eating *chametz.* Some believe it is derived of the name Maimon, the father of the Rambam, Rabbi Moshe Ben Maimon, and the Mimouna marks the date of his birth or death.
After settling in Israel, Jewish immigrants from North Africa (Maghrebim) celebrated the Mimouna with their families. Since 1966 it has been a national holiday.

The celebration begins after nightfall on the last day of Passover. Moroccan and Algerian Jews open their homes to visitors who are welcome to enjoy a lavish spread of traditional holiday cakes and sweetmeats.

The table is also laid with various symbols of luck and fertility, with an emphasis on the number "5," such as five pieces of gold jewelry or five beans arranged on a leaf of pastry. 5 represents: harmony and balance, it is the symbol of the universe, characteristics of man: 5 fingers, toes, 5 senses, etc.

In Israel, Mimouna is a popular holiday with outdoor parties, picnics and barbeques.

CHAPTER SEVEN

COUNTING THE OMER

"Even unto the morrow after the seventh sabbath shall ye number fifty days... "
Leviticus 23:16

In ancient times, the first sheaf of barley was harvested at the end of the first day of Pesach, after sundown (the beginning of a new day for the Jewish people). Orthodox Jews continue this practice even today. The barley was brought to the Temple as a thank offering. From that day onwards, the barley could be harvested and used.

After harvesting the first sheaf, 49 days were counted, and on the 50th day, *Shavuot* (= weeks) began. This also heralded the beginning of the wheat harvest. By "counting the Omer", the two major agricultural events were connected with each other. The Omer is a Biblical measure of volume of grain.

During their wanderings in the desert, the Israelites received the Torah on Mount Sinai, on the day of *Shavuot.*

Today, many observant Jews use the period of the Counting of the Omer to prepare themselves spiritually for the second pilgrim festival. It is a time of semi-mourning in which they don't shave, cut their hair, listen to music, conduct weddings, or attend parties and dinners with dancing.

According to the Talmud, 12,000 pairs of Torah study partners died during Roman occupation – either because of a plague, or because of Roman oppression. On *Lag Ba'omer* (33rd day of Counting the Omer) the plague lifted (or the rebellion saw a victory), which is celebrated in Israel with great bon-fires. Things that were first prohibited can now be enjoyed to the full.

Some people use this time of mourning to remember Jews who were murdered during the Crusades, pogroms and blood libels that occurred in Europe during the Middle Ages.

INTRODUCTION TO ISRAEL'S MEMORIAL DAYS

Israel's memorial days commence a week after the end of the *Pesach* holiday. These are:

- *Yom Hashoah* - Holocaust Remembrance Day
- *Yom Hazikaron* - Remembrance Day
- *Yom HaAtsma'ut* - Independence Day

"...lest thou forget the things which thine eyes have seen, and lest they depart from thy heart all the days of thy life: but teach them thy sons, and thy sons' sons; "
Deuteronomy 4:9

To Forget Means to Die – to Remember, to Live

Zechor! Remember!
The active verb is described by Webster as "something that is kept alive in the memory, so that it can be called to conscious thought without effort."
Recalling/recollecting implies some effort or will to bring something back to mind. To reminisce is to remember, to tell others of past events or about your personal experiences.

Zachar (zechor) is the Hebrew word for remember, think of, mention.
Genesis 8:1 says that *"God remembered Noah."* The LORD tells Noah in Genesis 9:15, *"I will remember my covenant",* and gave us the rainbow to remind us of His promise to mankind. God acts in remembrance of His covenant promises. He remembered Abraham, His people. *"I heard their groaning... remembered My covenant..."* Exodus 6:5-6
God's promise to remember was repeated by the covenant he made on Mount Sinai, when the Israelites became a people. We read this in Leviticus 26:40-45. Psalm 98:3; 105:8; 42; 106:45 also mention the fact that God remembers His covenant.
In Ezekiel 16:60 God remembers His promise to restore His people and bring them back from captivity. Jeremiah 31:34 says, *"I forgive their iniquity, I will remember their sin no more."*

God commands His people to:
"Remember this day when you came out of Egypt." Exodus 13:3
"Remember the Sabbath day." Exodus 20:8
Above all, *"to remember His marvelous works."* Psalm 105:5; 1 Chronicles 16:15

Zikaron means remembrance, memorial.
God said of His covenant name (YHWH = LORD) *"this is my memorial unto all generations"* (Exodus 3:15; Psalm 30:4; 135:13). The name recalls His acts to fulfil His Covenant. God's people were commanded to *"remember Amelek."* (Exodus 17:14).

The bronze layer that covered the altar (Numbers 16:40) and the heap of stones near the Jordan River (Joshua 4:7; 20-24) served as perpetual memorials to the sons of Israel. Two "memorial stones" inscribed with the names of the twelve tribes were part of the priest's ephod.
Before the Israelites went into battle, the people sacrificed sheep and trumpets were blown. *"May they be a memorial before your God."* Numbers 10:9-10

The Greek word *anamimnesko* is used in an active voice, and means to remind, call to ones mind. *Anamnesis* is remembrance. The word is still used today by doctors when referring to the patient's medical history.
Those suffering from *amnesia* are forgetful and have difficulty remembering.

When celebrating communion, Christians are told to *"Do this in remembrance of Me!"* 1 Corinthians 11:24-25

For the Jewish people, remembrance is an integral part of their lives.

The practice of lighting memorial candles in memory of deceased relatives is based on Proverbs 20:27, *"The spirit of man is the candle of the Lord."*

Originating from medieval Germany, the practice spread to other communities. Because memorial lights must burn 24 hours, special candles are used in metal or glass holders.

Memorial services and their special prayers (*Hazkarah*) remember the dead and express the hope their souls may be granted eternal repose. We read about this ancient practice in 2 Maccabees 12:43. Judah Maccabbee tells the people, *"... to pray for the dead and make atonement for them, so that they might be cleared of their sin."* In Talmudic times these *hazkarot** had become accepted customs.

In Judaism, remembrance is seen in a positive light. It doesn't inflict guilt or exact vengeance, but evokes positive action in light of the negative things that have befallen someone. That is why Jewish hospitals have walls with names of donors honoring the memory of a loved one.

For many people, national memorial days are heart wrenching because of the traumatic memories they evoke. Mourning is an integral part of Judaism. However, in order to sit *shiva**, there first has to be a burial. Imagine the agonizing situation a family faces when their child goes missing in action, or is kidnapped by Israel's enemies. The Jewish people are willing to pay a high price in order to bring their (dead) children home.

ROSEMARY AND REMEMBRANCE

Rosemary shrubs can be found all over Israel. A member of the mint family, the evergreen shrubs have a pungent aromatic fragrance. The ancient people already knew about its reputation for strengthening the memory. Modern day scientists have proven that Rosemary's scent is an effective memory stimulant.
Paul says in 2 Timothy 2:8, *"Remember that Jesus Christ.... was raised from the dead."*
Yeshua, our Savior, rose from the dead. He is the Source and supplier of all our needs. Christians should never forget God's goodness towards His people.
Not only the Jewish people, but Christians too, should: **Remember! And live!**

CHAPTER 9

DEATH AND BURIAL CUSTOMS IN ISRAEL

The Jewish attitude towards death is a combination of defiance and acceptance. Life is to be cherished and preserved, and death is to be fought. No effort should be spared to save a dying person. To die on your birthday, is seen as a special blessing from God - only very special people die on their birthdays.

When someone has died at home, the body is placed on the floor with his/her feet towards the door. The eyes and mouth are closed and the body covered with a sheet.
A candle is lit and placed near the head.

From the moment of death till the burial, the body of the deceased is not to be left alone. Often, the family arranges for a *shomer**, someone to sit by the deceased and recite psalms.

In Talmudic times, the announcement of death had to be made indirectly, by blowing the *shofar.* The man who summoned the congregation to early morning prayers in the synagogue, usually knocked three times on the doors or windows; when he knocked only twice, people knew someone had died.

Today, family members inform each other about the death of a loved one and let them know at what time the burial will take place - usually within 24 hours.

BAYIT KEVAROT (place of graves), or *Bayit Olam** - House of Eternity - Cemetery.
The area of a Jewish Cemetery is considered holy and only reserved for Jewish burials. Some cemeteries have separate rows for men and women and different communities - e.g. Ashkenazim and Sephardim.
Non-Jews are buried in their own cemeteries or special sections.

***KEVURAH* - BURIAL** (The internment of the dead)
In ancient Israel, leaving a corpse unburied was considered to be a horrifying indignity (See 1 Kings 14:11). It was a religious obligation to bury the dead - even criminals who had been hanged. (See Deuteronomy 21:23.)
It was seen as a curse when someone's remains fell prey to the birds, and there was no one to frighten them off. (See Deuteronomy 28:26.)

Most Jewish communities have their own *Chevrah Kadisha** (lit. Holy Brotherhood) or burial society who prepares the body for burial by ceremonial washing. In order not to discriminate between rich and poor, all people were and are to be buried in a shroud.
Common practice since 200 AD, this custom continues in Israel; Diaspora Jews are often buried in a plain, wooden casket.
In Israel, people are buried without a casket and covered only by the *kittel** and *tallit.*

Women are buried in white shrouds only. At the funeral, mourners traditionally rend an outer garment, a ritual known as *keriah**. This garment is worn throughout shiva* (mourning period).

Burial is considered as providing a final measure of atonement for the deceased. As with a *genizah**, Jews bury things as an honorable "internment," and would only burn things as a means of destruction.

*Halacha** (Jewish law) forbids cremation. Because the Nazis cremated thousands of Jews during the Holocaust, cremation is seen as an even more negative connotation.

Today, in Israel it is generally accepted to lay flowers on a grave, but some Diaspora communities see it as a gentile custom.

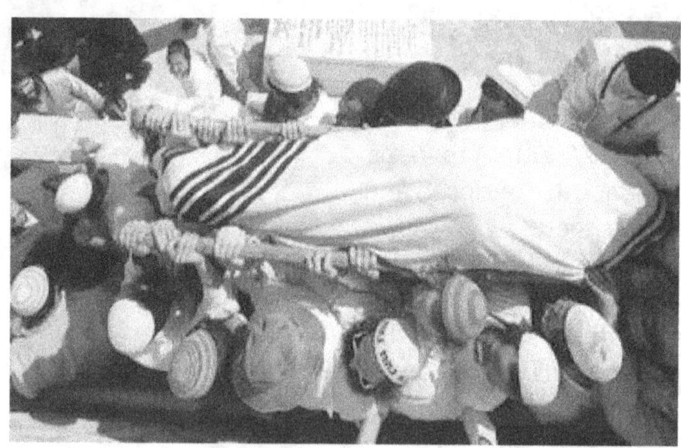

SUPERSTITIONS

- Many people believed that the angel of death wiped his bloody knife in water near the dead, hence all water jars in the courtyard of the house had to be poured out on the ground.
- Because *shedim* (spirits) followed the dead to their grave, and hovered around them, the funeral cortège had to wash their hands before entering the house - it wasn't enough to dip them in the river. (Hence a special sink at the cemetery.)
- In order to drive away the spirits that followed the mourner, people had to sit down and rest several times.
- The board upon which the dead person had been ceremonially washed, could not be turned over.
- One should not visit the same grave twice on the same day, and should not sleep in the cemetery.
- People were advised not to look closely on the face of a dead person, nor kiss the dead, not even when it was a relative.
- A dying child could be released from death's grasp if its parents 'sold' it to a friend for a shekel.
- A change of name may save from death.
- Removal of a feather pillow from beneath the head of a dying person helped the soul to depart more easily. (Some rabbis objected to this practice, as they believed it hastened death.)
- It is a good omen to die with a smile on the face, or to die on one's birthday.
- Rain on the day of a funeral is seen as a sign of compassion and forgiveness toward the dead.

CHAPTER 10

MOURNING CUSTOMS

Shiva (lit. seven) is the week-long mourning period in Judaism for first-degree relatives: father, mother, son, daughter, brother, sister and spouse.
The tradition developed from Genesis 50:1-14 in which Joseph mourns the death of his father Jacob for seven days.

The mourning period, also called "sitting *shiva**," begins immediately after burial, which in Israel has to take place within 24 hours.
Boys older than 13, and girls older than 12 years old are expected to mourn for a close family member. The Jewish laws on mourning balance emotionalism and philosophic wisdom.

Mourners are expected to cry, tear their garments and participate in the burial ceremony. However, they are not allowed to mourn too much or for too long. The emphasis of the mourning period is to recover from the loss and to focus on the business of living.

Aninut * (intense mourning) is the first stage of mourning, when someone is in total shock and disoriented. *Aninut* lasts until the burial is over and is followed by *Avelut* * (mourning). An *avel* (mourner) does not listen to music or go to concerts, and does not attend any joyous events or parties such as weddings, *Bar or Bat Mitzvahs,* unless absolutely necessary.

Shiva – Seven days
For seven days, family members receive visitors (except on *Shabbat* and on a *Yom Tov** (holiday). In observant households, a minyan assembles at the mourner's house for a Torah reading.
Traditionally, the first meal after the funeral, the *seudat havra'ah** (meal of comforting), is supplied by neighbors or friends.

Mourners do not bathe or shower, they do not wear leather shoes or jewelry and men do not shave. In many communities household mirrors are covered. Marital relations and Torah study is not permitted. (Mourners can study the laws of mourning, and read Bible portions that are connected to *Tisha B'Av.*)

It is customary for the mourners to sit on low stools, or even the floor, symbolizing the fact they are "brought low" by grief.

It is considered a great *mitzvah** (literally "commandment" but usually interpreted as "good deed") of kindness and compassion to visit a house in mourning. Because mourners are not allowed to serve food to the visitors, family and friends take care of the guests, the cooking and cleaning.

Traditionally, no greetings are exchanged and visitors wait for the mourners to initiate conversation, or remain silent if they keep quiet, out of respect for their bereavement.
Visitors are expected to talk about the deceased and share stories of his or her life. Some mourners use the *shiva* as a distraction from their loss, others prefer to grieve together with friends and family.

Upon leaving an (Ashkenazi) shiva house, visitors recite a traditional blessing: *"May God comfort you among the other mourners of Zion and Jerusalem."*

Depending on the customs, others may add: *"You should have no more tza'ar (distress)"* or *"You should have only simchas (celebrations)"* or *"we should hear only besorot tovot (good tidings) from each other"* or *"I wish you a long life"*. At a Sephardic shiva, visitors say: *"May Heaven comfort you."*

No one goes to a house of mourning during the *Shabbat* or holidays. On these days, mourners wear their festive clothes, pray in synagogue, but do not lead services.

If the first day of a *Yom Tov* (holy days which include *Rosh Hashanah, Yom Kippur, Sukkot, Pesach and Shavuot*) occurs during shiva, the mourning period ends and the remainder of shiva is cancelled. (Even if a *Yom Tov* begins at nightfall on the day of the funeral.) Burials never take place on a *Yom Tov.*

In Israel, mourners only return to work after the *shiva*. After the death of a parent, one is considered a mourner for twelve months.

SHLOSHIM – THIRTY DAYS

The thirty-day period following burial (including *shiva)* is known as *shloshim* (thirty). During this period, a mourner is forbidden to marry or to attend a religious festive meal. Men do not shave or get haircuts during this time.

Shloshim marks the end of the mourning period for other relatives than parents and spouse. On the eve of the *Shloshim* it is traditional for families to share support, recite prayers and Psalms, and to give charity in the merit of the deceased.

Towards the end of the 19th century the ritual of the unveiling of the tombstone became popular. In Israel, the unveiling of the headstone is done after the *shloshim*. At the end of the ceremony, a close family member removes the cloth covering. Usually, the service includes a brief eulogy for the deceased.

SHNEM-ASAR CHODESHIM - THE TWELVE MONTHS

Mourners who lost a parent observe a twelve-month period counted from the day of death. During this period, most activity returns to normal, although mourners continue to recite the mourner's *kaddish* for eleven months. They are not allowed to attend festive occasions and large gatherings where live music is played.

HAZKARAH AND YAHRZEIT

Hazkarah is the last memorial service of the first 12 months of mourning. The *Yahrzeit* ((Yiddish, "time of year") refers to the anniversary of the day of death of a relative. This is usually commemorated by lighting a memorial candle at home and visiting the grave, where a family member recites the *Kaddish* and the *El Maleh Rachamim* prayer. (See next page.)

In Biblical times, graves were marked with mounds of stones. By placing (or replacing) them, the visitor helped maintain the gravesite.

When visiting a Jewish grave, it is custom to place a small stone on the slab with the left hand. It shows others visited the gravesite, and participated in the *mitzvah* of burial.

Traditional honorifics for the dead which are used when naming and speaking of the deceased. The most common one is *zikhrono li-vrakha"* (m.) *"zikhronah livrakha"* (Of blessed memory) It is often abbreviated in English both as OBM and as *"Z"L"*. The Hebrew abbreviation is ז״ל.

KADDISH

(Lit. sanctification) is an Aramaic prayer of praise to God. Originally it was a brief prayer in synagogue. The mourner's *Kaddish* became accepted practice in the 13th century, at the time of the Crusades. From the 15th century, the prayer began to be used as a recitation on the anniversary of the death of a family member. *Kaddish* can be recited both by men and women, including non-religious Jews.

"Glorified and sanctified be God's great Name throughout the world which He has created according to His will. May He establish His kingdom in your lifetime and during your days and within the life of the entire house of Israel, speedily and soon. Blessed and praised, glorified and exalted, extolled and honoured, adored and lauded be the Name of the Holy One blessed be He, beyond all the blessings and hymns, praises and consolations that are ever spoken in the world, and let us say Amen."

EL MALEH RACHAMIM

This prayer probably dates from the Chmielnicki massacres in Eastern Europe (1648-1649)

"O God, full of compassion, Who dwells on high, grant a perfect rest on the wings of the Divine Presence - in the exalted places among the holy and the pure ones who shine like the brightness of the firmament - to the soul of … who has gone to his (her) eternal repose [and for whose sake… will make a contribution to charity in solemn remembrance].
May his (her) resting place be in the Garden of Eden. May the Compassionate One shelter him (her) forever in His protective wings and may his (her) soul be bound up in the bond of eternal life. The Lord is his (her) inheritance; may he (she) rest in peace, and let us say: Amen."

CHAPTER 11

YOM HASHOAH -
HOLOCAUST REMEMBRANCE DAY

In the week following *Pesach*, Israeli flags appear on government buildings and balconies of homes in preparation of *Yom Hazikaron laShoah ve-laG'vura* ("Holocaust and Heroism Remembrance Day). This day is generally known as *Yom Hashoah* (Holocaust Remembrance Day, or Holocaust Day).

It commemorates the six million Jews who perished during the Holocaust by the hand of the Nazis. Since 1953 it is a national memorial day, held on the 27th of Nisan (April/May). When it falls adjacent to Shabbat the date is shifted by a day.

Most Jewish households light memorial candles and many recite *Kaddish** (the prayer for the departed).

On the eve of *Yom Hashoah* and the day itself, places of public entertainment are closed by law. Israeli television airs Holocaust documentaries and Holocaust-related talk shows, and low-key songs are played on the radio. Flags on public buildings are flown at half mast.

In Israel, *Yom Hashoah* opens at 8 p.m. in a state ceremony held in Warsaw Ghetto Square at Yad Vashem, the Holocaust Martyrs' and Heroes Museum, Jerusalem. There is no siren that evening. During the ceremony, the national flag is lowered to half-mast, followed by speeches from the President and the Prime Minister. Holocaust survivors light six torches symbolizing the six million Jews who perished in the Holocaust and the Chief Rabbis recite prayers.

The next day, at 10:00 a.m., a two-minute siren (the 'all clear' sign) sounds throughout Israel. People stand at attention, cars stop and drivers stand next to their cars. Most of the country comes to a standstill as many people pay silent tribute to the dead.
On *Yom Hashoah,* nationwide ceremonies and services are held at schools, military bases and other public places.

*Ner Zikaron ** - Memorial Light

This is a special lamp or light kindled in memory of a departed relative. The practice comes from Proverbs 20:27 - *"The soul of a man is a lamp for the Lord"*. The tradition probably originated in medieval Germany. Besides *Yom hashoah and Yom Hazikaron,* memorial lights are kindled on three other occasions: during the *Shiva*, the *Yahrzeit* of a family member and on the evening of *Yom Kippur.*

CHAPTER 12

YOM HAZIKARON - REMEMBRANCE DAY

Yom Hazikaron is a memorial day of those who have fallen since 1860 (when Jews first began to live outside the walls of Jerusalem's Old City). It usually falls on the 4th of Iyar (often in May). If the date falls on a Friday or Saturday, the celebrations are moved up.
Since 1963, *Yom Hazikaron* has become Israel's official memorial day on which fallen soldiers and victims of terror are remembered.

Memorial services open at 8 p.m. with a one-minute siren. Nationwide memorial services are attended by Israel's top leadership and military personnel. The main ceremony takes place at the IDF cemetery on Mount Herzl, Jerusalem.

The following day, a two-minute siren sounds at 11 a.m., marking the opening of official memorial ceremonies and private gatherings at cemeteries where soldiers are buried.
Again, traffic comes to a standstill, and people stand with bowed heads in honor of the fallen soldiers.

The day officially draws to a close between 7–8 p.m. with the opening ceremony of Israel's Independence Day on Jerusalem's Mount Herzl, when the Israeli flag is returned to full staff.

Scheduling *Yom Hazikaron* right before Y*om Ha'atzmaut* is intended to remind people of the price paid for independence, and what was achieved with the sacrifice of the soldiers. Many Israelis have served in the IDF, or are connected to those who were killed during Israel's military conflicts.

Israel's Memorial Day - *Yizkor Prayer*

May God remember the souls of His heroic children: The fighters of the Israeli Defense Forces, who fell in the wars of Israel, in defensive, retaliative, and security actions and during the fulfilment of their duty, including the souls of the underground fighters and brigades who fought in the nation's struggle - all those who sacrificed their lives for the sanctification of God's Name.

And with the help of God, the Lord of Israel's campaigns, they brought about the revival of the nation and the state and the redemption of the land and the city of God.

They were quicker than eagles and stronger than lions as they volunteered to assist the nation, and they saturated our holy land with their pure blood. The memory of their self-sacrifice and heroic deeds will never disappear from us.

May their souls be bound in the Bond of Life with the souls of Abraham, Isaac and Jacob, and with the souls of the other heroes and martyrs of Israel who are in the Garden of Eden.

Amen

The National Flag
and Emblem of Israel

Degel Yisrael (the flag of Israel) was adopted on October 28, 1948, five months after the country's establishment. It depicts a blue Star of David on a white background, between two horizontal blue stripes.

The basic design recalls the Tallit, the Jewish prayer shawl, which is white with blue stripes.

- The star in the center is the *Magen David* (Shield of David).
- White: Symbol of light, honesty, innocence and peace.
- Blue: symbolizes trust, loyalty, wisdom, confidence, intelligence, faith, truth, and heaven.

This flag, adopted by the first Zionist Congress in Basle in 1897, had become accepted by Jewish communities throughout the world as the emblem of Zionism and it was thus natural to use it at the official proclamation of statehood.

The Austrian Jewish poet Ludwig August Frankl (1810-1894) was the first person in modern times, who voiced the idea that blue and white are the national colors of the Jewish people.

More than three decades before the First Zionist Congress, Frankl published a poem entitled "Judah's Colors".

Not only did the new State of Israel require a national flag, it also needed an official emblem to demonstrate its sovereignty in the community of nations.

The Israeli emblem was adopted nine months after the State was established.

It symbolized the continuity and fulfilment of the Zionist dream in the emblem of Israel. Zechariah's vision (Zechariah 4:1-3; 11-14) of the menorah and olive branches represents the Zionist idea of the newly established State of Israel.

It corresponds to the rebuilding of the Temple in Jerusalem after the Return to Zion. The two olive trees represent "religion" and "state" (the "two anointed dignitaries" - the high priest and the governor) stand together to realize the Zionist dream.

CHAPTER 13

YOM HA'ATZMAUT -
INDEPENDENCE DAY

Yom Ha'atzmaut is celebrated on the 5th day of Iyar in the Hebrew calendar. On this day, David Ben-Gurion publicly read the Israeli Declaration of Independence. The corresponding Gregorian date was 14 May 1948. Should the 5th of Iyar fall on a Friday or Saturday, celebrations are moved to the preceding Thursday.

Yom Ha'atzmaut begins around 8 p.m. with an official opening on Jerusalem's Mount Herzl, which is broadcast live on television. The ceremony includes a speech by the speaker of the Knesset (the Israeli Parliament), artistic performances, (forming elaborate structures such as a Menorah or *Magen David*) and the ceremonial lighting of twelve torches, one for each of the Tribes of Israel.

The Torch lighters are Israeli citizens who made a significant social contribution to a specific area.

Many cities hold outdoor performances in its squares, featuring leading Israeli singers and fireworks displays. In order to allow people to sing and dance, many streets and squares are closed to cars.

The following day, a flyover of combat planes and IDF helicopters start off the main activities of Independence Day. The president, IDF chief of staff, Prime minister and Defense minister sing their favourite Independence Day songs with the IDF band and singers.

Later that day, Israel's President honors 120 excellent IDF soldiers at his official residence in Jerusalem.

Other activities which take place on *Yom Ha'atzmaut* are:

⇒ International Bible Contest in Jerusalem
⇒ Israel Prize ceremony in Jerusalem
⇒ The IDF opens some of its bases to the public
⇒ Israel Defense Forces Parade (1948-1973)
⇒ Hebrew Song Contest (1960–1980)

All over the country, Israeli families flock to the parks to have picnics and barbecues, (known as *mangal* in Israeli slang.) The word comes from the Arabic word for stove.
Balconies and buildings are decorated with Israeli flags, and small flags are attached to car windows. Many Israelis keep their flags displayed until *Yom Yerushalayim* (Jerusalem Day).

Because the Chief Rabbinate declared *Yom Ha'atzmaut* a Jewish holiday, observant Jews recite Hallel (Psalm 113-118) during services.

Some Haredim (Ultra-Orthodox) join the crowds and enjoy a barbecue. However, ultra-Orthodox Jews who are members of the Satmar, Toldos Aaron, Toldos Avraham Yitzchak, and Neturei Karta sects do not celebrate Yom Ha'atzmaut. They claim that the establishment of a Jewish state before the coming of the Messiah is a sin. Some even fast on this day and recite prayers for fast days.

AL HA NISSIM (For the Miracles)

This prayer of thanksgiving was composed in the Talmudic era. It is recited during the Amidah, grace after meals, and the *Chanukah and Purim* holidays. Some communities link the text with the War of Independence (1948).

"We thank You for the miracles,
the redemption, the mighty deeds,
and the saving acts You performed,
as well as for the wars which You did wage,
for our fathers in days of old at this season."

Israeli Druze, Bedouins and Circassians usually celebrate Israel's independence. The majority of Arabs living in Israel however, regard Israel's Independence day as a tragic day in their history. They call it *al-Nakba* (the catastrophe).

GOOD TO KNOW

The opening ceremony of *Yom haAtsma'ut* on Mt. Herzl can only be attended by invitation. You can try to obtain a ticket to attend the dress rehearsal the week before.
The evening street parties in Jerusalem are an experience you won't forget. People 'hit' each other on the head with large inflatable hammers. Don't wear your best clothes, as you may be 'sprayed' with foam!

CHAPTER 14

LAG BA'OMER

Lag Ba'omer (also known as *Lag La'Omer* amongst Sephardic Jews) is celebrated on the 33rd day of the Counting of the Omer, which occurs on the 18th day of the Hebrew month of Iyar. (Usually in May.)

According to the Talmud, 24,000 students of Rabbi Akiva died from a divinely sent plague during the Counting of the Omer. In the years that followed, Jews began to celebrate the end of the plague on *Lag Ba'omer.*

Rabbi Akiva continued with only five students,  amongst them Rabbi Shimon bar Yochai, who became the greatest teacher of Torah in his generation.

Akiva decided his students should learn to fight the Roman conquerors. To avoid suspicion, they dressed up as hunters carrying bows and arrows, and went to the woods to practice. Eventually, the students joined the Bar Kochba rebels in their fight for freedom.

During the Roman Empire, the Romans believed it was unlucky to marry in May, before the harvest. They believed that the souls of the dead came back to earth at that time to haunt the living, and would only be appeased by funerals, not weddings. This period lasted 32 days, and ended with a festival on the 33rd day. The Roman practice coincided with the Jewish practice of Counting of the Omer, which ended with *Lag Ba'ome*r, on the 33rd day.

In the Middle Ages, *Lag Ba'omer* became a special holiday for rabbinical students. On this so-called "Scholar's Day," it was customary to practice outdoor sports.

In ancient times farmers used to worry (they actually still do) during the Counting of the Omer, whether the new grain crops would succeed or fail. Israeli spring weather is always unstable. Hot desert winds (*sharav*) can dry out the seedlings or burn the standing grain. Another danger is locusts, other insects or plant diseases. Until the farmer knows the outcome of his respective harvests, he is not in the mood for private or public celebrations.

While the Counting of the Omer is a semi-mourning period for observant Jews, all restrictions of mourning are lifted on the 33rd day of the Omer. Amongst Ashkenazi Jews, weddings, parties, listening to music, and haircuts are commonly scheduled to coincide with this day. Sephardi Jews marry on *Lad Ba'omer,* the 34th day of the Omer.

On the eve of the holiday, huge bonfires are lit all over the country. Children often begin to collect wood after the Pesach holiday.

Some believe that the practice of having these bonfires goes back to the days  of Bar Kochba, who lit fires in Jerusalem to signal to other villages and towns that they had captured the capital. In turn, the villages kindled fires which could be seen even further away.

The following day, families enjoy picnics and outings into the woods. Children continue to play with bows and rubber-tipped arrows.

The Meron celebrations date from the time of Rabbi Isaac Luria (1534-1572). Since then it became customary to give three-year-old boys their first haircuts (*upsherin**) during *Lag Ba'omer.*

Zionist ideology connected *Lag Ba'omer* to the Bar Kochba revolt against the Roman Empire. The holiday became a symbol for the fighting Jewish spirit.

The Gadna program (youth brigades) of the IDF (Israel Defense Forces) was established on Lag Ba'omer in 1941. Their emblem bears a bow and arrow.

On *Lag Ba'omer* 1948, the Israeli government ordered the establishment of the Israel Defense Forces.

In 2004, *Lag Ba'omer* was named as the day to salute the IDF reserves.

UPSHERIN

Upsherin (Yiddish Upsherinish (lit. shear off) or *chalaka*) is a Jewish haircutting ceremony, Kabbalistic in origin, held when a Jewish boy is three years old. The *upsherin* tradition is (for Judaism) relatively modern and has only been traced back as far as the 17th century.

R. Yehudah Leibush Horenstein, a Chassidic rabbi who emigrated to Ottoman Palestine in the middle of the 19th century writes that "this haircut, called *chalaka*, is done by the Sephardim in Jerusalem at the *kever* (grave) of Shimeon bar Yochai during the summer, but during the winter they take the boy to the synagogue or *Bayit Midrash* and perform the haircut with great celebration and parties, something unknown to the Jews in Europe." Because there was no Hebrew or Yiddish name for the custom, it was called by the Yiddish word for cutting off the hair: "*upsheren*".

In the Chassidic community, the *upsherin* marks a male child's entry into the formal educational system and the commencement of Torah study.

From now on, it will wear a *kippah** (yarmulke) and *tzitit**. The child will be taught to pray and read the Hebrew alphabet. So that Torah should be "sweet on the tongue," the Hebrew letters are covered with honey, and the child licks them as he reads.

Some communities weigh the hair that is cut off in the *upsherin* ceremony, and give the amount to charity. If the hair is long enough, it may be donated to a charity that makes wigs for cancer patients. Other customs include having guests snip off a lock of hair, and encourage the child to put a coin in a *tzedakah** box for each lock that is cut.

Cutting hair is not allowed during the time of the Counting of the Omer, but is permitted on *Lag Ba'omer.* This is why boys who turned three between *Pesach and Lag Ba'ome*r celebrate *upsherin* on this date.

The biggest Lag Ba'omer celebrations are held at the tomb of Rabbi Shimon bar Yochai in Meron, in the Galilee. Shimon bar Yochai was a famous 1st-century tannaic sage in ancient Israel, active after the destruction of the Second Temple in 70 CE. He was one of the most eminent disciples of Rabbi Akiva, and is attributed with the authorship of the Zohar, the chief work of Kabbalah*.

During the time of Rabbi Isaac Luria (1534-1572), parents used to distribute wine and sweets while their son had his first haircut. This custom is still popular today. Rabbi Isaac Luria. a Jewish mystic from Safed in the Galilee region of Ottoman Palestine is considered the father of contemporary Kabbalah.

Today, many orthodox Jews travel to Mount Meron to celebrate their son's *upsherin*. Jerusalemites who cannot travel to Meron, hold celebrations at the grave of Shimon Hatzaddik.

The Bible sometimes compares human life to the growth of trees. Leviticus 19:23 states that one is not permitted to eat the fruit that grows on a tree for the first three years.

Some Jews apply this principle to cutting a child's hair, and therefore only at the age of three does the child get its first haircut.

Chassidic Jews hope that the child, like a tree that grows tall and eventually produces fruit, will grow in knowledge and good deeds, and someday have a family of his own.

Some communities call a boy before his first haircut an *orlah* - the same word used for a tree in its early years.

THE KIPPAH ~ YARMULKE

A *kippah (*plural *kippot*) is a head covering that observant Jewish males wear to show their respect for God.

The Talmud states, *"Cover your head in order that the fear of heaven may be upon you."* Rabbi Hunah ben Joshua never walked 4 cubits (2 meters) with his head uncovered. He explained: *"Because the Divine Presence is always over my head."*

According to the *Shulchan Aruch**, Jewish men are strongly recommended to cover their heads, and doing so, should not walk more than four cubits bareheaded. Covering one's head, such as by wearing a kippah, is described as "honoring God".

In the Middle Ages in Europe, the distinctive Jewish headgear was a full hat with a brim and a central point or stalk. Originally used by choice amongst Jews to distinguish themselves, some Christian governments made it compulsory as a discriminatory measure.

In the early 19th century in the United States, rabbis often wore a scholar's cap (large saucer-shaped caps of cloth, like a beret) or a Chinese skullcap. Other Jews of this era wore black pill-box-shaped *kippot.*

In many communities, boys are encouraged to wear a *kippah* from a young age in order to ingrain the habit.

The color and fabric of the *kippah* can be a sign of adherence to a specific religious movement. Knitted or crocheted *kippot*, known as *kippot serugot*, tend to be worn by Religious Zionists and the Modern Orthodox, who also wear suede or leather *kippot*.

Bucharan *kippot* are popular with children, and also worn by liberal-leaning, feminist and reform Jews.

Yemenite *kippot* are typically black velvet with a 1–2 cm. embroidered strip around the edge having a multi collared geometric, floral or paisley pattern.

Members of most Haredi groups usually wear black velvet or cloth *kippot*. In general, the larger the kippah, the more traditionalist the wearer. By contrast, the smaller the *kippah*, the more modern and liberal the person is.

In Jerusalem you sometimes find men wearing a full-head-sized, white crocheted *kippah*, sometimes with a knit pom-pom or tassel on top. Don't confuse Muslim men (who sometimes wear a similar looking '*kippah*') with Jewish followers of the late Rabbi Yisroel ber Odesser. The phrase *"Nach Nachma Nachman Me'uman"* is crocheted in or embroidered on the *kippah*.

Modern *kippot* have different colors of sports teams, especially football.

Kippot have been inscribed on the inside as a souvenir for a celebration (*bar/bat mitzvah** or wedding).

There are specific *kippot* for women.

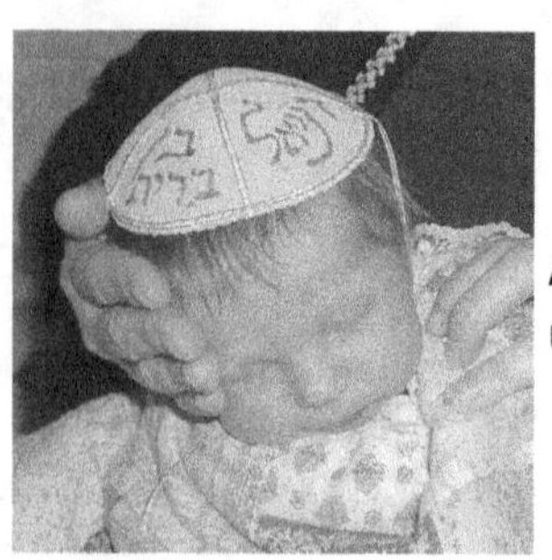

A special baby *kippah* with two strings on each side to fasten it, is often used for a *brit milah** ceremony.

CHAPTER 15

YOM YERUSHALAYIM
JERUSALEM DAY

Yom Yerushalayim is a national holiday commemorating the reunification of Jerusalem and the establishment of Israeli control over the Old City in June 1967. In the aftermath of the 1948 War of Independence, Jerusalem was a divided city for 19 years. Israel's capital was reunited during the 1967 Six Day war.

On May 12, 1968, the government proclaimed a new holiday—Jerusalem Day. It was to be celebrated on the 28th of Iyar, the Hebrew date on which the divided city of Jerusalem became one. (Usually May or beginning of June.) On March 23, 1998, the Knesset passed the Jerusalem Day Law, making the day a national holiday.

The Chief Rabbinate of Israel declared Jerusalem Day a minor religious holiday to thank God for victory in the Six-Day War and for answering the 2,000-year-old prayer of *"Next Year in Jerusalem"*.

The day is marked by state ceremonies, memorial services for soldiers who died in the battle for Jerusalem and parades through downtown Jerusalem.

In synagogues, congregants recite the *Hallel** prayer and other blessings.

Israeli schools teach the children about the significance of Jerusalem, and hold festive assemblies. This day is also marked in Jewish schools around the world.

Jerusalem, the capital of Israel, has become a large and expansive city. From all over the world, tourists come to see her beauty, to learn about her past and make pilgrimage to the holy sites. Jerusalem is a connecting point for the three major religions - Judaism, Christianity and Islam.

On June 7, 1967, the day Jerusalem was liberated, Defense Minister Moshe Dayan declared:

"This morning, the Israel Defense Forces liberated Jerusalem. We have united Jerusalem, the divided capital of Israel. We have returned to the holiest of our holy places, never to part from it again. To our Arab neighbors we extend, also at this hour—and with added emphasis at this hour—our hand in peace. And to our Christian and Muslim fellow citizens, we solemnly promise full religious freedom and rights. We did not come to Jerusalem for the sake of other peoples' holy places, and not to interfere with the adherents of other faiths, but in order to safeguard its entirety, and to live there together with others, in unity."

This declaration is still relevant today.

SAYINGS ABOUT JERUSALEM

- *"If I forget thee, O Jerusalem, let my right hand forget her cunning."* Psalm 137:5
- Fair-crested, joy of all the earth.
- Ten measures of beauty descended on the world; Jerusalem took nine and the rest of the world, one.
- A city that joins all Jews together because they are all partners in her.
- All who pray in Jerusalem are as though they pray before the Divine throne.
- When Jerusalem was destroyed even God went into mourning and there will be no joy before Him until it is rebuilt and Israel returns into its midst.
- When a Jew prays, he must mention Jerusalem.
- Jerusalem has 70 names, including City of David (2 Samuel 5:9), Lion of God (Isaiah 29:1); City of God (Psalm 87:2); City of Truth (Zechariah 8:3); Joyful City (Isaiah 22:2); Faithful City (Isaiah 1:26); and Paragon of Beauty (Lamentation 2:15).

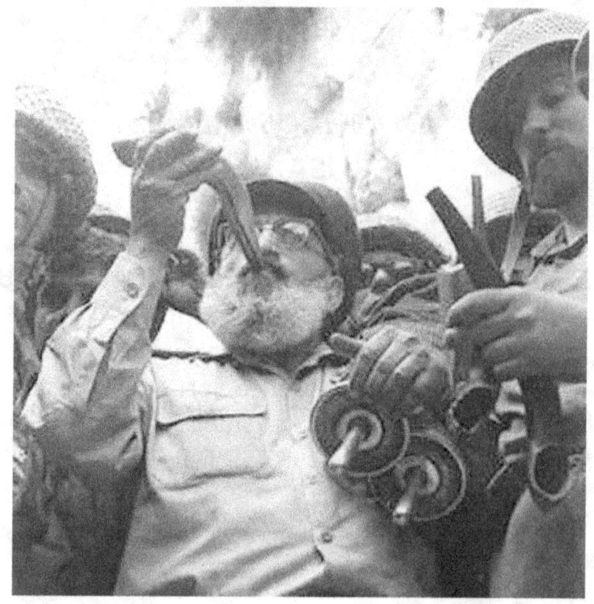

GOOD TO KNOW

On Jerusalem Day, the so-called 'Parade of the Flags' is held. Usually beginning at Sacher Park, the happy participants (mostly religious young people) sing and dance their way to the Old City. The parade ends at the Kotel. Buy a flag and join the crowd!

CHAPTER 16

SHAVUOT - THE FEAST OF WEEKS

In Israel, *Shavuot* is celebrated only for one day - on the 6th day of the Hebrew month of Sivan (Usually late May, beginning of June.) In the Diaspora, Jews celebrate it for two days. The Christian holiday of Pentecost always falls on the 7th Sunday after Easter.

"… when thou art come in unto the land which the Lord thy God giveth thee for an inheritance, and possessest it, and dwellest therein; That thou shalt take of the first of all the fruit of the earth, which thou shalt bring of thy land that the Lord thy God giveth thee, and shalt put it in a basket, and shalt go unto the place which the Lord thy God shall choose to place his name there…" **Deuteronomy 26:1-3**
"And thou shalt observe the feast of weeks, of the firstfruits of wheat harvest, and the feast of ingathering at the year's end."
Exodus 34:22

The Hebrew word for *Shavuot* means "weeks" and refers to the counting of seven weeks from the second day of the *Pesach* (Passover) holiday. This period is called the "Counting of the Omer". *Shavuot* is the only Pilgrim festival of which the Bible doesn't give a specific date on which to celebrate.

Different names of *Shavuot*

- *Chag Shavuot* (Festival of Weeks)
- *Chag ha Katsir* (Reaping holiday)
- *Yom ha Bikkurim* (day of first fruits)
- Pentecost (Greek for 50)

About seven weeks after their departure from Egypt, the Israelites received the Torah on Mount Sinai. Upon their arrival in the Promised Land, 40 years later, *Shavuot* became connected to the grain harvest. Harvest time begins during *Pesach* with the barley harvest, and ends with the wheat harvest at *Shavuot*. The harvesting season was usually one of gladness.

In ancient times, Jewish farmers brought their first fruits to the Tabernacle in Shiloh. In the First and Second Temple period, they brought their baskets to the Temple in Jerusalem. *Bikkurim* (first fruits) had to be from the "seven species" – wheat, barley, grapes, figs, pomegranates, olives and dates.
(Deuteronomy 8: 7-8)

When the first fruit appeared, the farmer would tie a reed around the fruit and declare, *"This is a first fruit."*

Preparing to go up to Jerusalem for pilgrimage, the rich people placed their fruits in golden or silver baskets, while the poor used baskets from peeled willow-shoots. Oxen pulled carts which were heavy laden with the baskets. The horns of the animals were gilded and laced with garlands of flowers.

From all over the country people travelled to appointed cities, where a local assembly-head was responsible for the pilgrims. In order not to become ritually unclean, people did not enter the houses but slept in the streets.

At dawn the pilgrims set out together - towards Jerusalem, dancing and singing, *"I was glad when they said unto me, Let us go into the house of the Lord."* Psalm 122:1. Upon entering the city, the pilgrims would joyously sing, *"Our feet shall stand within thy gates, O Jerusalem."* Psalm 122:2 Jerusalemites welcomed them with, *"Our brothers from …, welcome and peace to you!"* Carrying the baskets on their shoulders, (even the king had to carry his own basket), the people presented their offerings to the priests.

When a pilgrim presented his basket to the priest, he had to recite, *"A Syrian ready to perish was my father, and he went down into Egypt…"* Deuteronomy 26:5 The baskets became property of the priest and Levites, who represented the "firstborn" sons of the Israelites. Standing side by side, rich and poor rejoiced in all the good things the LORD their God had given to them and their households. (See Deuteronomy 26:11)

Bikkurim has the same root as *bechor* (first

born). The first of everything belonged to God – man and animal alike. Israel was God's "firstborn", and in recognition of His ownership of the land and His sovereignty over nature, the first grain and fruits had to be offered to Him.

In the Temple, the Levites ground the wheat into fine flour, from which leavened "twin loaves" were baked and eaten by the priests. This was the only time that leaven was used, for all other grain offerings had to be sacrificed and burned unleavened.

During *Shavuot*, trumpets and flutes were played before the altar. *"Also in the day of your gladness, and in your solemn days, and in the beginnings of your months, ye shall blow with the trumpets over your burnt offerings, and over the sacrifices of your peace offerings; that they may be to you for a memorial before your God…"* Numbers 10:10

After the destruction of the First and Second Temple, the main emphasis shifted to the anniversary of receiving the Torah on Mount Sinai. Because the first fruits could not be offered anymore, rabbis suggested replacing it with charity. In the Middle Ages it became tradition to start the formal Jewish (religious) education of young children around the time of *Shavuot*.

The Book of Jubilees (also called the *Leptogenesis*, the "lesser Genesis") is parallel to Genesis and parts of Exodus. Between 1947 and 1956, fifteen Hebrew "Jubilee scrolls" were found at Qumran. Probably written between 135-105 BC, these scrolls were well known by early Christian writers and rabbis. The book of Jubilees associates *Shavuot* with the Covenant and Torah and the Covenants God made with Noah and Abraham as an offering of first fruits.

Oriental Orthodox churches still consider the Book of Jubilees an important part of the Bible. The book traces the first *Shavuot* to the appearance of the first rainbow – the day God made a covenant with Noah. Other apocrypha books, Tobit and II Maccabees, also mention the "Feast of Weeks".

Modern-day (Ashkenazi) *Shavuot* Celebrations

According to this stream in Judaism: Torah must be *reshit* (first). This is linked to a set of customs, whose first letters form the word *"acharit"* (last). Thus there is:

1. *Akdamot*
2. *Chalav* (milk)
3. Ruth
4. *Yerek* (greenery)
5. Torah

1. *Akdamot* - a liturgical poem, read in synagogue. It is written by Rabbi Meir bar Yitzchak of Worms (Germany), whose son was murdered during the Crusade of 1096.
2. *Chalav* - milk. The Rabbis reasoned that because the Israelites didn't have time to prepare meat for *Shavuot*, they only consumed dairy products. It's a popular custom to eat cheese cake and *blintzes* (pancakes filled with cheese) during *Shavuot*.
3. Ruth. After the morning service, the scroll of Ruth is read in synagogues because it describes the harvest periods and how Ruth became a member of the Jewish people by accepting the Torah. Converts to Judaism are honored at this time. Tradition tells us that King David (form the line of Boaz and Ruth) was born and died on *Shavuot*. Many people visit his grave on Mount Zion in Jerusalem during the holiday.

4. *Yerek* - greenery. Homes and synagogues are decorated with greenery. The *bimah** (platform) where the Torah readings take place now looks like a *chuppah** (wedding canopy). Moses, the matchmaker, brought the Jewish people (bride) to the *chuppah* (Mount Sinai) to marry the bridegroom (God). The Torah was the *ketubah** (wedding contract).
5. Torah study. The custom of all-night Torah study was initiated in 1533 by a Greek Kabbalistic rabbi. Hourly subjects are taught by a different teacher and 'the night passes like a dream'.

Morning prayers are recited at first light, followed by the chanting of the Ten Commandments. In honor of King David's birth and death on *Shavuot*, his psalms are also read.

In the 1890's, secular *Shavuot* celebrations were introduced by the kibbutzim (collective farms). Being agricultural communities, the first fruits of the produce of each kibbutz was presented to the community and guests in a festive ceremony.

Later, factory products began to receive a place of honor in the parades. But the highlight always was (and still is) when the parents proudly present their 'crop' of newborn babies to the community.

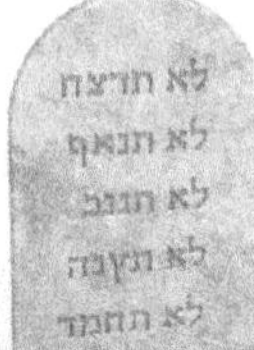
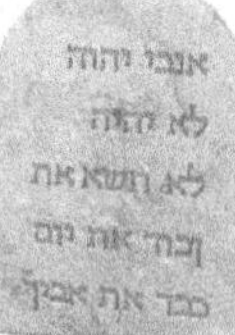

The Land of Israel,
The blessing of its soil,
Embraced the home of the Jew
Wherever he dwelt.

Abba Kovner

The fast of the Seventeenth of Tammuz (*Shiv'ah Asar b'Tammuz*) is usually the end of June, beginning of July. The minor fast day commemorates the destruction of the Ten Commandments by Moses; it also laments the breach of the walls of Jerusalem before the destruction of the Second Temple.
It marks the beginning of the three-week mourning period leading up to *Tisha B'Av.*

CHAPTER 17

Tisha b'Av – The Ninth of Av

The 9th day of Av usually falls in the middle of the summer holiday, in August.
On this solemn day, the Jewish people commemorate the destructions of their Temples by fasting 24 hours and praying. In Israel, most restaurants and places of entertainment are closed on this day.

Throughout the ages, *Tisha b'Av* has been a black day in Jewish history.
The *Mishnah* mentions specific events which took place:

- On this day, the twelve spies returned to Moses; ten of them with bad news about the Promised Land.
- In 586 BC, Nebuchadnezzar destroyed Solomon's Temple and sent the Judeans into Babylonian Exile.
- In 70 AD, the Second Temple was destroyed by the Romans, and the people in Judea scattered. It heralded the beginning of the Jewish exile from Eretz Yisrael.
- 135 AD, Bar Kochba's revolt against the Romans was crushed and Betar destroyed.

In later years, more *Tisha b'Av* disasters were added to the list of commemorations.
On this day:

- All Jews were expelled from England in 1290
- The Jews from Spain were expelled in 1492.
- The same fate awaited the Jews from Vienna, whose turn came in 1670.
- World War I officially began on the 9th of Av in 1914, when Germany declared war on Russia.

In the period between the 17th of Tammuz (July) till the 9th of Av, (August), religious Jews don't eat meat, drink no wine (except for *Shabbat*), do not wear new clothes, and do not schedule happy events, such as weddings and house dedications. The 25 hour fast begins at nightfall on the 9th of Av.

In the synagogue, the Ark housing the Torah scrolls is draped in black and the lights are dimmed. Wearing only socks or slippers, no (leather) shoes, people sit on the floor or on low stools. Like true mourners, they don't greet each other with *"Shalom"*.
Torah study is forbidden, for this is considered to be a joyful activity. During this fast day, the book of Lamentations, Job and parts of Jeremiah are read in the synagogue.
Special mourning prayers, *kinot* (written during the Middle Ages) are also recited.

Orthodox Jews believe that when Messiah comes, Tisha b'Av will be a day of celebration instead of mourning.

> *"Thus saith the Lord of hosts; The fast of the fourth month, and the fast of the fifth, and the fast of the seventh, and the fast of the tenth, shall be to the house of Judah joy and gladness, and cheerful feasts; therefore love the truth and peace."*
> **Zechariah 8:19**

A religious Jew will never throw away his old prayer book, or discard a Torah Scroll. These are kept in a special place (*Genizah**) and are usually buried on *Tisha b'Av*.

CHAPTER 18

Tu b'Av

Tu b'Av, the 15th (*Tet = 9, Vav = 6*; 9+6=15) of the Hebrew month of Av, is one of the lesser known holidays in the Jewish calendar. It has gained popularity since the establishment of the State of Israel.

Coming less than a week after the sorrowful mourning of *Tisha b'Av, Tu b'Av* is the Jewish holiday of love. Like Chanukah, Purim and *Tisha b'Av,* it is a rabbinic (post-biblical) addition to the holiday calendar. *Tu b'Av* occurs on a full moon, and therefore is linked with love, fertility, and romance.

The first mention of *Tu b'Av* is in the *Mishnah*,* where it says, *"There were no better days for the people of Israel than the Fifteenth of Av and Yom Kippur, since on these days the daughters of Jerusalem go out dressed in white and dance in the vineyards. What they were saying: Young man, consider who you choose (to be your wife)."* (Taanit 4:8). According to Rabban Shimon ben Gamliel (10 BC - 70 AD), on this day the "tribes of Israel were permitted to mingle with each other".
The holiday was instituted in the Second Temple era to mark the beginning of the grape harvest, which ended on Yom Kippur.

The Talmud mentions other *Tu B'Av* commemorations:
- On either the 14th or 15th of Av, the Pharisees (rabbinic Jews) were victorious over the Sadducees.
- Members of the Tribe of Benjamin were readmitted to the community.
- The death of the generation that left Egypt ended.

- King Hosea, of the Northern Kingdom, removed the restrictions of King Jeroboam prohibiting the northerners to make pilgrimages to Jerusalem.
- The Romans permitted the Jews to bury their dead who had fallen at Beitar.

In Biblical times, brides-to-be danced in Shiloh, a community in Samaria, which was the first capital of Israel.

Today, Jews have returned to the vineyards of Shiloh. Again, unmarried girls dance in the vineyards serenaded by song.

Tu b'Av, the day of love, is a popular date for Jewish weddings. Even though it is a regular workday, music and dance festivals are held throughout the country.

Israelis send cards and flowers to their loved ones. These customs are observed by all segments of Israeli society, whether they consider themselves religious or non-religious.

> **GOOD TO KNOW**
>
> The community of Shilo in Samaria hosts special events during *Tu B'Av,* which include walking tours to Tel Shiloh, the site where the Tabernacle stood.

CHAPTER 19

THE HIGH HOLY DAYS

"Speak unto the children of Israel, saying, In the seventh month, in the first day of the month, shall ye have a sabbath, a memorial of blowing of trumpets, an holy convocation." Leviticus 23:24-25

The Hebrew month of Elul (August/September) is the month of the "High Holy Days". The period between *Rosh haShana* (Jewish New Year) and *Yom Kippur* (Day of Atonement) is also called "the ten days of awe", because of the need for introspection and repentance.

Rosh haShana (lit. head of the year) heralds the Hebrew month of Tishrei (September/ October) Tishrei is Aramaic for "to begin". It is celebrated for two days and is seen as a Day of Judgment. On the first day, the *tashlich** ("you will cast") ritual takes place in which "sins" are symbolically cast into open water. People also throw bread and pebbles.

Rosh haShana is a day of rest, like the *Shabbat.* The sound of the *shofar** (ram's horn) is intended to awaken people from their "slumber" and alert them to the coming judgment.

The days of repentance begin with *Rosh haShana* and climax at *Yom Kippur.* Religious Jews believe that even though judgment is pronounced on *Rosh haShana,* during the following ten days they can mend their ways and alter judgment in their favor. (That is why people are extra nice to each other.)

In the weeks leading up to the holiday, people greet each other with *"Shana Tova"* (A good year) or *"Shana Tova uMetuka"* (A good and sweet New Year). Often they add *"Gmar Chatima Tova"* (May you be inscribed in the Book of Life), referring to the coming *Yom Kippur*, Day of Atonement.

Apple and honey, symbolizing the sweet New Year is always part of the holiday cuisine. Other symbolic food is a fish head ("head" of the new year) and a round *challah,* to symbolize the year cycle).

In ancient times, *Rosh haShana* was the beginning of the economic year. The emphasis was on the agricultural seasons and the pilgrim's festivals (*Pesach, Shavuot and Sukkot).* It those days it was only celebrated for one day, instead of the modern two-day holiday.

Rosh haShana is seen as the anniversary of God's Creation. On this day, mankind passes before the Creator, like sheep before the shepherd. Three books are opened – the Book of Life, which seals the righteous, who will live; The wicked are *"blotted out of the book of the living"* (See Psalm 69:29), while those "in between" have until *Yom Kippur* to repent and become righteous.

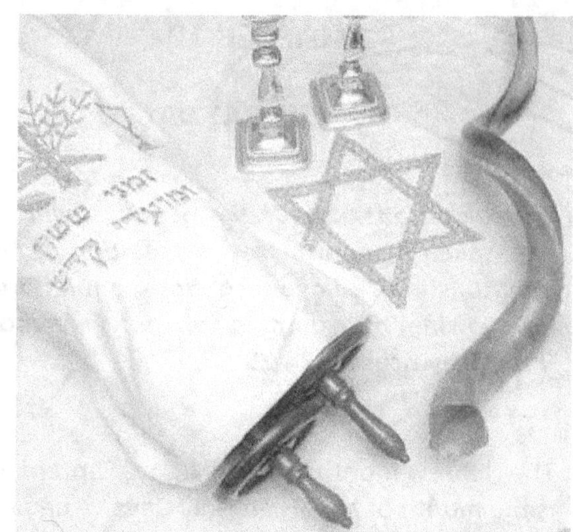

SEFER HACHAIM - THE BOOK OF LIFE

"And the Lord said unto Moses, Whosoever hath sinned against me, him will I blot out of my book." Exodus 32:33

In Judaism (and Christianity) the Book of Life (*Sefer Hachaim)* is the book in which God records the names of every person who is destined for Heaven.
According to the Talmud, the Book of life is opened on *Rosh Hashanah* together with the Book of the Dead, where the names of the wicked are recorded. Many Old Testament references are given to the Book of Life. To be blotted out of God's Book of Life signifies death.

The Psalmist speaks of the Book of Life in which only the names of the righteous are written: *"Let them be blotted out of the book of the living, and not be written with the righteous."* Psalm 69:28
Even the tears of men are recorded in this Book of God:
"Thou tellest my wanderings: put thou my tears into thy bottle: are they not in thy book?" Psalm 56:8

The Book of Life is probably identical with the Book of Remembrance in which the deeds of those that fear the Lord are recorded.

The Book of Jubilees 30:20-22, speaks of two heavenly tablets or books:
"...a Book of Life for the righteous, and a Book of Death for those that walk in the paths of impurity and are written down on the heavenly tablets as adversaries (of God)."

In the New Testament, the Book of Life is referred to six times.
"And whosoever was not found written in the book of life was cast into the lake of fire." Revelation 20:15.

ROSH HASHANA

The word *Rosh haShana* is not mentioned in the Torah. Leviticus 23:24 calls it "day of blowing horns (*shofarim*)".
Ezekiel 40:1 calls it *"the beginning of the year"; while in rabbinic literature they call it "day of judgment" and "day of remembrance".*

DIFFERENT "NEW YEARS"

◊ 1st of Nissan (March/April) - "Biblical New Year" after the Exodus from Egypt. Determined the length of a king's reign and start of the ecclesiastical Calendar.
◊ 1st of Elul (August/September) – Beginning of the year to tithe animals for the Temple.
◊ 1st of Shevat (January/February) – this later changed to the 15th (*Tu beShevat)* and was called the "New Year of Trees". Calculations were made for the tithes of the fruit harvest.
◊ 1st of Tishrei (September/October) – civil Hebrew Calendar, and beginning of legal contracts.
◊ 1st January – New Year on the Gregorian Calendar.

SHOFAR

In Biblical times, the sounding of the shofar heralded the beginning of a *Rosh Chodesh* (new month). It was also used as a warning sign of danger and to proclaim the inauguration of a new king. The shofar is symbolic of Abraham's sacrifice of Isaac, in which the ram became the substitute sacrifice. The curved horn symbolizes man's bowing in submission before God.

On both days of *Rosh haShana*, the *shofar* is blown 100 times in synagogue and has three distinct sounds:

♦ **Shevarim** - resembles sobbing
♦ **Teruah** – nine staccato notes resembling wailing
♦ **Tekiah** – unbroken long sound

Many orthodox men wear a *kittel** (Yiddish). This white robe is also worn by a bridegroom, symbolizing purity. The same robe is often used as a burial shroud. (Isaiah 1:18 says that *"Our sins shall be made as white as snow."*) It is a reminder of the white linen robe the High Priest wore during Temple ceremonies. People visit the graves of loved-ones and pray for a good year.

*Tzedekah** (charity) is a way of Jewish life, and an integral part of *Yom Kippur.* Especially during the holiday season people donate money to many charitable organizations.

Rosh Hashanah Blessings

"May it be Your will, Lord our God and the God of our fathers, that we be filled with mitzvot like a pomegranate [is filled with seeds]."

"May it be Your will, Lord our God and the God of our fathers, that You renew for us a year good and sweet like honey."

Rosh Hashanah Seder

The *Rosh Hashanah Seder* is conducted at the beginning of the *Rosh Hashanah* evening meal. The goal of the Seder is to help those at the table to move closer towards repentance. Before each food is eaten, a specific prayer is recited.

On a special plate are specifically chosen food, whose Hebrew names are related to other Hebrew words that convey wishes for the coming year.

- Dates - "May our enemies be consumed."
- Black eyed beans - "May our merits multiply."
- Leeks - "May our enemies be decimated."
- Beets - "May our adversaries be removed."
- Gourd (Squash) - "May the Lord tear up our evil sentence."
- Pomegranate - "May we be filled with mitzvoth like the pomegranate (which is filled with seeds)."
- Apple (cooked in sugar) and honey - "May the Lord renew for us a good and sweet year."
- Head of a sheep/ram or a fish - "May we be the head and not the tail."

THOUGHTS ON *TZEDAKAH* - CHARITY

⇒ A person must be scrupulous in fulfilling the commandment to give charity, for this is the sign of a descendant of Abraham.

⇒ Israel will be redeemed through acts of charity.

⇒ As great as is the commandment of charity, even greater is persuading another to give charity.

⇒ Charity is one of the things whose profits man enjoys in this world, but whose principal remains for the world to come.

⇒ Charity is equal to all the other commandments combined.

⇒ Everyone should give charity; even he who depends on charity should give to those who are even less fortunate.

⇒ It is better not to give charity than to do so and shame the recipient publicly.

⇒ He who is generous to the poor makes a loan to the Lord. Nobody is ever impoverished through giving charity.

⇒ Do not humiliate a beggar: God is beside him.

TASHLICH ceremony

*Tashlich** (casting off) is a long-standing Jewish practice which is still performed on the first afternoon of *Rosh Hashanah*. When it falls on a *Shabbat*, the ceremony is postponed to the next day. The custom is derived from Micah 7:18-20, *"You will cast all their sins into the depths of the sea."* (KJV)
Though *Tashlich* is not mentioned in the Talmud, its earliest reference appears in Nehemiah 8:1, *"All the Jews gathered as one in the street that is in front of the gate of water."* (KJV) This gathering is known to have taken place on *Rosh Hashanah.*

Tashlich is usually performed on the first day of *Rosh Hashanah,* but may be performed up until *Hoshanah Rabba* (the last day of *Sukkot*), except on *Shabbat*. Special verses are recited next to a body of water, such as a sea, river, stream, lake or pond, preferably one that has fish. When these were not available, some rabbis are known to do *Tashlich* next to a well, even one that dried up, or next to a bucket of water.
The men shake out the corners of the *tallit katan*, or the pockets of their coats or pants.

The goal of *Tashlich* is to cast both their sins and the Heavenly prosecutor (Satan) into the Heavenly sea. Shaking their clothes after the *Tashlich* prayer is a tangible act to achieve the spiritual goal of shaking sins from their souls.

The practice varies in different countries. E.g. Jews in Kurdistan enter the water in order to be cleansed from sins.
Polish Chassidim used to put straw floats in the water and set them afire.
They believed their sins were symbolically carried away and burnt up.

Tsom (Fast of) Gedalia

Tsom Gedalya (the Fast of Gedalia), on the 3rd of Tishrei (after *Rosh haShana*), is to lament the assassination of the righteous governor of Judah- Gedalia. This tragic event ended Jewish rule following the destruction of the First Temple. (See Jeremiah 41.) *"But it came to pass in the seventh month, that Ishmael the son of Nethaniah, the son of Elishama, of the seed royal, came, and ten men with him, and smote Gedaliah, that he died, and the Jews and the Chaldees that were with him at Mizpah. And all the people, both small and great, and the captains of the armies, arose, and came to Egypt: for they were afraid of the Chaldees."*
2 Kings 25:25-26

CHAPTER 20

Yom Kippur – Day of Atonement

"And the Lord spake unto Moses, saying, Also on the tenth day of this seventh month there shall be a day of atonement: it shall be an holy convocation unto you; and ye shall afflict your souls, and offer an offering made by fire unto the Lord. And ye shall do no work in that same day: for it is a day of atonement, to make an atonement for you before the Lord your God." **Leviticus 23:26-28**

Yom Kippur falls on the 10th of Tishrei (Usually September/ October).

During Temple times, a week before *Yom Kippur, the Cohen Hagadol* (High Priest) went to live in his chamber in the Temple in order to prepare himself spiritually and physically for this holy day. On *Yom Kippur* he was to make atonement for all Jews in the world. This was the only time of the year he entered the Holy of Holies.

During the *Avodah* (lit. work, the Temple service) the high Priest had to change his garments five times - each time a different set of clothing. He also immersed himself five times in the *mikveh**, washed his hands and feet ten times, sacrificed two lambs, one bull, two goats, and two rams. He offered meal and wine libations, and made three incense offerings.
On this day, he had to work harder than all the priests and Levites that were on duty.

Today, Orthodox Jewish men immerse themselves in the *mikveh** (ritual bath) the day before Yom Kippur. The ultra-orthodox (Haredim) have a custom called *kapparot** on the morning before *Yom Kippur*.

While reciting Bible verses relating to redemption, a live fowl is swung over the head.
The fowl is then given to the poor. Many rabbis reject this superstitious custom. (A circle is like a magic ring to ward off evil spirits.)

Early in the afternoon, all Jewish businesses and shops are closed, and traffic virtually comes to a stand still. Traffic lights stop working and there is no national radio or television. Even Ben Gurion International Airport closes its airspace to all air traffic in the early afternoon. About four hours after the end of the holiday the airport reopens for international arrivals. Departures commence an hour later. Likewise, all harbors and border crossings in and out of the country close for the holiday. As a security measure, the crossings into Gaza, Judea and Samaria are also closed until the end of this holiest day of the year.

Just before sunset, the streets fill with people walking to nearby synagogues. Children with bicycles or skate boards take over the main roads.

In synagogues around the world, the cantor chants the Aramaic *Kol Nidrei** (all vows). This prayer dates from post-Talmudic times and the music is composed mid 15-16th century in south Germany.
"May all the people of Israel be forgiven, including all the strangers who live in their midst, for all the people are in fault..."

Through the *"Kol Nidrei"* people ask God forgiveness for vows they made to God and people, but could not carry out.
"Al Chet" is the great confession of sins. (For prayers, see page 63.)

During the Middle Ages, German Jews replaced the *Kol Nidrei* with recitations of Psalms, because anti-Semites accused them of being not trustworthy. The belief that Jewish oaths were worthless, spurred many a pogrom.
During the Spanish Inquisition, when Jews forcibly were converted to Christianity, this stirring and haunting melody became even more relevant.

The Day of Atonement is the climax of the so-called *Yamim Nora'im** (days of Awe).
As a symbol of purity many Jews wear white clothing and either walk on plastic shoes or house slippers, as long as they are not from leather. Many people spend most of *Yom Kippur* in synagogue, where five prayer services are followed by litanies and petitions of forgiveness.

Throughout the day, the following Scriptures are read in synagogue:

♦ Leviticus 16:1-34
♦ Numbers 29:7-11
♦ Leviticus 18:1-30
♦ Isaiah 57:14-58:14
♦ Micha 7:8-20
♦ The book of Jonah

Even many non-religious Jews try to keep the 25 hour fast. During this holiest day of the Jewish Year, synagogue attendance usually triples.

When the sun is setting, many flock to the synagogue for the *Ne'ilah** prayer, after which the *Shema Israel* (see next page) is recited and the shofar blown. This symbolizes the closure of God's books, in which the names are written for those who shall live or die the next year.

For many centuries, it was customary to herald the end of *Yom Kippur* by blowing the *shofar* at the Western Wall in Jerusalem. This custom was re-installed in 1967 when Jerusalem was re-unified.

Most people break their *Yom Kippur* fast with a festive meal. Soon, the sound of hammers can be heard all over the city, as many religious Jews begin to build their *Sukkah** (tabernacle), for the Feast of Tabernacles.

Yom Kippur 5777

Holiday begins:	Holiday ends:
Jerusalem: 17:35	Jerusalem: 18:46
Tel Aviv: 17:52	Tel Aviv: 18:48
Haifa: 17:44	Haifa: 18:46
Be'er Sheva: 17:53	Be'er Sheva: 18:48
Safed: 17:44	Safed: 18:44
Eilat: 17:43	Eilat: 18:48

GOOD TO KNOW

The Great Synagogue on King George Street in Jerusalem is a good place to experience the moving rituals and prayers of *Yom Kippur*. Visitors are allowed to sit in the back. Neighborhood synagogues sometimes welcome visitors, but not all have Hebrew-English prayer books.
Dress modestly, don't wear leather shoes, and leave your handbag/backpack at home.

SHEMA YISRAEL - HEAR, [O] ISRAEL

The *"Shema Yisrael"*, often shortened to the *"Shema"* is a prayer that serves as a centerpiece of the morning and evening Jewish prayer services. *Shema Yisrael* comprises of Deuteronomy 6:4-9; 11:13-21 and Numbers 15:37-41. The three portions relate to central issues of Jewish belief. The *"Shema"* is one of the Old Testament sentences quoted in the New Testament.

"The first of all the commandments is, Hear, O Israel [Shema Israel]; The Lord our God is one Lord: And thou shalt love the Lord thy God with all thy heart, and with all thy soul, and with all thy mind, and with all thy strength: this is the first commandment." Mark 12:29-30

- **Shema** — listen, or hear and do or accept
- **Yisrael** — Israel, in the sense of the people or congregation of Israel
- **Adonai** — often translated as "LORD", and read in place of YHWH
- **Eloheinu** — the plural 1st person possessive of Elohim (our God). **Adonai**
- **Echad** — the cardinal number one

Observant Jews teach their children to say the *"Shema"* before they go to sleep at night. When the famous Rabbi Akiva was tortured to death, he recited the *Shema*, and used his last breath to say *"Echad"* (one). Since then, it has been tradition for Jews to recite the *Shema* when knowing they are going to die.

Sh'ma Yis'ra'eil Adonai
Eloheinu Adonai Echad
Hear, Israel, the Lord is
our God, the Lord is One

KOL NIDREI - ALL VOWS

"All vows, and prohibitions, and oaths, and consecrations, and konams and konasi and any synonymous terms, that we may vow, or swear, or consecrate, or prohibit upon ourselves, from the previous Day of Atonement until this Day of Atonement and from this Day of Atonement until the Day of Atonement that will come for our benefit.
Regarding all of them, we repudiate them. All of them are undone, abandoned, cancelled, null and void, not in force, and not in effect.
Our vows are no longer vows, and our prohibitions are no longer prohibitions, and our oaths are no longer oaths."

AL CHET - FOR THE SIN (excerpt)

These are the opening words of the "great Confession of Sins" recited nine times on *Yom Kippur*. Each line starts with the words *"Al Chet"* - "For the sin..."

"For the sin we have committed before You under duress or of our own free will. And for the sin we have committed before You by hardening our hearts. For the sin we have committed before You unwittingly. And for the sin we have committed before You with the utterance of our lips. For the sin we have committed before You by unchastity. And for the sin we have committed before You whether in public or in private..."

CHAPTER 21

SUKKOT - THE FEAST OF TABERNACLES

> *"And ye shall take you on the first day the boughs of goodly trees, branches of palm trees, and the boughs of thick trees, and willows of the brook; and ye shall rejoice before the Lord your God seven days... ye shall celebrate it in the seventh month. Ye shall dwell in booths seven days..."* **Leviticus 23:40-44**

Sukkot begins on the 15th of Tishrei, the date of the first full moon after the autumnal equinox. (September/October.) During this "season of our rejoicing", the Jewish people eat their meals in a tabernacle or booth, covered with boughs but with the sky showing through in remembrance of the wanderings from Egypt to the Promised Land.

Sukkot (Feast of Tabernacles) is one of the three Pilgrim festivals ordained by God.
People had to go up to Jerusalem to celebrate the feast in the Temple.

"Three times thou shalt keep a feast unto me in the year. Thou shalt keep the feast of unleavened bread... in the time appointed of the month Abib... And the feast of harvest, the firstfruits of thy labours, which thou hast sown in the field: and the feast of ingathering, which is in the end of the year...Three times in the year all thy males shall appear before the Lord God." Exodus 23: 14-17

Being an observant Jew, Jesus too celebrated *Sukkot*.

"Now the Jews' Feast of Tabernacles was at hand... Then the Jews sought him (Jesus) at the feast, and said, Where is he? ... Now about the midst of the feast, Jesus went up into the temple and taught... In the last day, that great day of the feast, Jesus stood and cried, saying, If any man thirst, let him come unto me, and drink. He that believeth on me, as the scripture hath said, out of his belly shall flow rivers of living water." John 7: 2,11,14,37-38 (NIV)

The three pilgrim feasts - *Pesach* (Passover), *Shavuot* (Pentecost) and *Sukkot* (Tabernacles) have both historical and agricultural significance.

Because *Sukkot* occurred in the fall harvest, it was also observed as an agricultural event. Prayers for rain were also recited during this holiday.

In Israel, the first and last days are celebrated as a full holidays (like a *Shabbat*); The "Eighth Day of Solemn Assembly" is celebrated as *Simchat Torah* (Rejoicing of the Law). People are allowed to work during *Chol Hamo'ed** (intermediate days), but the festival framework is maintained. Schools are closed, and many families enjoy the holiday together by going on outings, visiting family or entertaining guests in their Sukkah.

Different Names Relating to the Festival

- *Chag Ha'asif* (Festival of the Ingathering of the crops)
- *Chag Hasukkot* (Festival of Tabernacles)
- *Chag* (The Festival) - a popular name with the rabbis, suggesting that Sukkot was the holiday par excellence.
- *Zeman Simchatenu* (The Season of our Rejoicing) - referring to the Bible's commandment to "be joyful".

Sukkot's observance involves "dwelling" in the sukkah. The concept of thanksgiving for the harvest remains central, symbolized by the fruits (real or artificial) that decorate the *sukkot (one sukkah, two sukkot).*

Some say the American Pilgrim fathers were influenced by the Jewish observance of *Sukkot,* from which Thanksgiving Day came.

An important symbolic item of the Festival is the *Arba'ah Minim** (Four Species). These are held together and waved at different points in the religious services. The four species consist of a *lulav* (palm branch), *etrog* (citron), *hadasim* (three myrtle twigs) and the *aravot* (two willow branches). Combined, these are called the *Lulav*.*

Bible Readings During *Sukkot*

- The unabridged Hallel (Psalm 113-118) recited each morning.
- Leviticus 22:26-23:44
- Numbers 29:12-31
- Zechariah 14:1-21
- 1 Kings 8:2-21
- Exodus 33:12-34:26
- Ezekiel 38:18 – 39:16
- The book of Ecclesiastes

Simchat Bayit Hasho'evah
Water Drawing Ceremony

> ***"Therefore with joy shall ye draw water out of the wells of salvation." Isaiah 12:3***

The ancient water drawing ceremony, is prescribed in Deuteronomy, and also mentioned in the *Mishnah**. During the Temple period, at the end of the first day of Sukkot, huge golden lamps were lighted in the courtyard of the Temple, illuminating the whole of Jerusalem. Using harps, lyres, cymbals, trumpets, and many other instruments, the Levites would lead the assembled Jews in song. The water drawing ritual began with dancing and rejoicing and continued on through the night. Pilgrims watched and participated in joyful celebration.

The next morning, many pilgrims accompanied a group of Levites and priests to Jerusalem's *Shiloah* (Siloam) pool.

They played musical instruments and sang biblical songs, such as the well-known *"You shall draw water with gladness out of the wells of salvation."*

After the water was drawn with a golden vessel, the happy throng went up again to the Temple, all the while singing and dancing.

Taking the golden vessel, the High Priest poured the water in one of two bowls with narrow spouts. The other bowl contained wine. The priest held the water bowl high up to the west (where the rains came from) and the wine bowl towards the east. The assembled pilgrims watched as the liquids dripped from the spouts like rain drops.

Each day, a group of pilgrims would descend to Motza, a small village near Jerusalem, to cut willow branches. These were used to decorate the Temple's altar. Each day the altar was circled once by people holding the lulavim* and saying Hoshanah prayers.

On the last day of Sukkot the altar was circled seven times, after which the willow branches were beaten till the leaves fell - representing rain drops.

It also symbolized the fact that willows absorbed a lot of water, but didn't produce edible fruit - it wasted water. Destroying the branches was a symbolic gesture of water preservation. Others believed the falling leaves symbolized the casting away of sins.

Today, special "water drawing" ceremonies continue to be held in Jerusalem during the intermediate days of *Sukkot*.

Simchat Bayit Hasho'evah gatherings of music and dance take place in synagogues, *yeshivas*, or places of study. Refreshments are served in the adjoining *sukkah.* In Orthodox circles, a partition separates men and women during the festivities, which begin late in the evening, and often last long into the night.

A chassidic interpretation looks to water's lack of flavor for inspiration. Flavor and taste go by the Hebrew word *ta'am* which can also mean "reason." Pouring water on the altar symbolized and celebrated the Jews' unconditional love for God and their pledge to serve God whether or not they fully understood the logic behind the commandments.

On the first seven days of the festival, a procession takes place around the synagogue, while the *Hoshanot* prayers are recited and hymns are sung. The *"hosha-na"* (Save us, we pray) reminds us of the ceremony during Temple times when daily circuits were made around the altar.

BIRKAT COHANIM

"The Lord bless thee, and keep thee: The Lord make his face shine upon thee, and be gracious unto thee: The Lord lift up his countenance upon thee, and give thee peace."
Numbers 6:24-26

*Birkat Cohanim** (the priestly blessing) takes place early Monday and Thursday morning of the intermediary days, at the Western Wall in Jerusalem's Old City. Hundreds of Cohanim (whose family name indicates they are of the priestly line of Aaron) give the Aharonic blessing from Numbers 6:24-26, while covered with their *tallits* (prayer shawls).

The priestly blessing or priestly benediction is also known as raising of the hands (*nesiat kapayim), or Dukhanen* (from the Yiddish word *dukhan* - platform - because the blessing is given from a raised rostrum).

On the seventh day of *Sukkot*, the *Hoshanah Rabbah** (the Great Hoshanah) takes place, traditionally marking the conclusion of the solemn season. (The so-called 'solemn days' refer to the period beginning with *Rosh HaShana* (the Jewish New Year), and also include *Yom Kippur* (the Day of Atonement).)

Ashkenazi Jews wear a *kittel** during this time, (Yiddish for "smock"). It is a loose wide vestment that is worn on solemn occasion and on High Holidays. White associates with atonement and purity.

On the eighth day, the Prayer for Rain is recited, essential for a fruitful year.
The prayers for rain commence during *Sukkot* and continue until *Pesach,* which coincides with the end of the rainy season in Israel.

DIFFERENT TYPES OF RAIN

a. The **Joreh** - first rain after the long, dry summer. Usually falls end of October, beginning of November. Always a reason for joy and gratefulness, as the fields now can be ploughed and prepared for next year's harvests.
b. **Geshem** - winter rains, usually pouring down between mid-December and March.
c. **Melkosh** - 'latter (spring) rains'. Needed for the barley and grain harvest.

PRAYER FOR RAIN

"And it shall come to pass, if ye shall hearken diligently unto my commandments which I command you this day, to love the Lord your God, and to serve him with all your heart and with all your soul, That I will give you the rain of your land in his due season, the first rain and the latter rain, that thou mayest gather in thy corn, and thy wine, and thine oil."
Deuteronomy 11:13-14

Jews and Gentiles Celebrating *Sukkot*

> *"And it shall come to pass, that every one that is left of all the nations which came against Jerusalem shall even go up from year to year to worship the King, the Lord of hosts, and to keep the feast of tabernacles. And it shall be, that whoso will not come up of all the families of the earth unto Jerusalem to worship the King, the Lord of hosts, even upon them shall be no rain."*
> **Zechariah 14:16-19**

According to the Bible, in the millennial Kingdom gentile nations will have to come up to Jerusalem to celebrate Sukkot in order to be blessed with rain. Even though it is not commandment now, many Christians celebrate the Feast of Tabernacles.

For over 30 years, Christians have come up to Jerusalem to celebrate the Feast of Tabernacles. The International Christian Embassy sponsors the yearly celebration which attracts thousands of people from around the world.

Sukkot Symbols

◊ The *sukkah* represents the human's fragile state and the need for God's Divine protection.

◊ All of the Four Species grow near water sources; the majority of them are able to recover after a fire.

◊ Observant Jews believe in the importance of being rooted in the Word and getting water from the Source. Even when experiencing "fires" in their lives, new shoots will grow from the seemingly devastated tree.

A JEWISH YEAR

The year number on the Jewish calendar represents the number of years since creation, calculated by adding up the ages of people in the Bible back to the time of creation. The Gregorian year 2012 corresponds with the Jewish year 5772.

Jews do not generally use the words "A.D." and "B.C." to refer to the years on the civil calendar because "A.D." means "the year of our Lord." (Yeshua). Instead, they use C.E. (Common/ Christian Era) and B.C.E. (Before Common Era).

GOOD TO KNOW

Immediately following *Yom Kippur*, people begin to erect *sukkah* frames on balconies, rooftops, courtyards and sidewalks.
The municipality provides palm leaves for the roofs. Everywhere you'll find stalls selling (Christmas) decorations for the *sukkah.*
A walk through Mea Shearim or other orthodox neighborhoods is an experience you'll enjoy.

Shmitah - the Sabbatical Year

> *"And six years thou shalt sow thy land, and shalt gather in the fruits thereof: But the seventh year thou shalt let it rest and lie still; that the poor of thy people may eat: and what they leave the beasts of the field shall eat. In like manner thou shalt deal with thy vineyard, and with thy oliveyard."*
> **Exodus 23:10-11**

God commanded the *Shmitah* year (or *sheviit* - seventh year) to be one of social justice and kindness to animals (Leviticus 25:1-7). It also was to be a *"Sabbath unto God"* (Leviticus 25:1-7) and a *"Sabbath for the land"*, in which it could renew itself. Debts are to be forgiven (Deuteronomy 15:1-6) and the impoverished given a chance to make a fresh start.

The Torah forbids the planting of trees and vegetables, pruning, and harvesting during the sabbatical year. However, trees can be irrigated if they would otherwise die.

The fruits and plants growing in fields during the sabbatical year are called *hefker**. They belong to no one and to everyone, and it is forbidden even to chase a wild animal away from the field if they want to eat. A Jew can eat fruit from a tree during the sabbatical year, but is not allowed to sell it or take a bundle home.

In Leviticus, God expressly promises that He will bless the sixth year with abundant produce if the people of Israel have faith enough to keep the sabbatical year. Not everyone had such faith. The Babylonian exile was directly connected to this failure to keep the sabbatical year. According to the Torah, during exile 'the land will have its Sabbath'.

During Talmudic times, it became increasingly difficult to keep the sabbatical year. Hillel (110 BC - 10 AD) instituted the *Prosbol* system, which meant that a creditor would appoint the court to collect his debts. Hillel was criticized for circumventing the law, which only applied to individuals.

When Jews returned to Israel after the *galut** (exile), the question of *shmitah* became relevant again. Before the sabbatical year of 1889, Jewish farmers received permission to sell their land to a non-Jew for the prescribed period, thus continuing to have it worked. Many orthodox authorities opposed this solution. Today, some orthodox farmers use hydroponics during the sabbatical year. (Hydroponics is a subset of hydroculture and is a method of growing plants using mineral nutrient solutions, in water, without soil.)

There are many Israeli farmers who observe *shmitah* to the full letter of the law without looking for *Halachic** loopholes. These farms remain completely idle, and bring in no revenue during the Sabbatical Year. Special funds are set up by kind donors to help the farmers observe this *mitzvah**. The year 5768 (2007-2008) and 5775 (2014-2015) were Sabbatical Years. The next *Shmitah* year will be in 5782 (2021-2022).

Hakhel Ceremony

"And Moses commanded them, saying, At the end of every seven years, in the solemnity of the year of release, in the feast of tabernacles, When all Israel is come to appear before the Lord thy God in the place which he shall choose, thou shalt read this law before all Israel in their hearing. Gather the people together, men and women, and children, and thy stranger that is within thy gates, that they may hear, and that they may learn, and fear the Lord your God, and observe to do all the words of this law: And that their children, which have not known any thing, may hear, and learn to fear the Lord your God, as long as ye live in the land whither ye go over Jordan to possess it."
Deuteronomy 31:10-13

*Hachel** refers to a custom based on the mandated practice in the Bible of assembling all Jewish men, women and children to hear the reading of the Torah by the king of Israel once every seven years.

Originally this ceremony took place at the site of the Temple in Jerusalem during *Sukkot* in the year following a Seventh Year. According to the *Mishnah**, the "commandment to assemble" was performed throughout the years of the First and Second Temple era. It was discontinued after the destruction of the Temple and the dispersal of the Jewish people from their land. In the twentieth century, however, it was revived by the government of Israel and by groups of observant Jews.

The first official Israeli ceremony of *Hakhel* was held during Sukkot of 1945, the year following the sabbatical year. Similar ceremonies presided over by Israel government officials have been held every seven years since. Sometimes the President of Israel performs the ceremony; other times, well known rabbis lead the ceremony at the Kotel (Western Wall) in Jerusalem.

YOVEL - THE YEAR OF JUBILEE

*Yovel** - the Jubilee year is the year at the end of seven cycles of *shmitah** (Sabbatical years). According to Biblical regulations this year had a special impact on the ownership and management of land in *Eretz Yisrael*. Some debate whether it was the 49th year (the last year of seven sabbatical cycles, referred to as the Sabbath's Sabbath), or whether it was the following (50th) year.

The sacred fiftieth year is a time of freedom and of celebration when everyone will receive back their original property, and slaves will return home to their families. (See Leviticus 25:10)

The biblical rules concerning Sabbatical years (*shmita*) are still observed by many religious Jews in Israel, but the regulations for the Jubilee year have not been observed for many centuries.

CHAPTER 22

SHEMINI ATZERET - SIMCHAT TORAH - REJOICING OF THE LAW

"I rejoice at thy word, as one that findeth great spoil." **Psalm 119:162**

Simchat Torah (Rejoicing of the Law) is celebrated on the eighth day of *Sukkot*. In the Diaspora it is celebrated a day later. *Simchat Torah* marks the conclusion of the annual Torah reading cycle and the beginning of a new one.

During Temple times, 70 sacrifices were offered during the seven days of *Sukkot* - more than on any other holiday. Some believe it was to be an act of gratefulness for a successful harvest that was coupled with a prayer for abundance in the upcoming year. Talmudic scholars believe that the 70 sacrifices were to bring merit to the proverbial 70 nations of the world. Today, congregants pray for the gentile nations.

Rabbis have tried to answer why God commanded an eighth day, even though He stipulated that *Sukkot* was only seven days. According to them, God asked His people to remain with Him for one more day.
The practice of the annual reading cycle was established between the sixth and eleventh century AD, and therefore is not mentioned in the Talmud.
In the Middle Ages, some communities lit bonfires, using the dismantled and disposable parts of the *sukkah.*

On the evening of *Simchat Torah,* all the Torah scrolls are taken out of the Ark* and carried around the *bimah** (reader's platform). This is the only night of the year that this is done.

During the seven-fold procession (*hakkafot**) a special chant is sung. Each procession is separated by an interlude of singing and dancing in which the people carrying the Torah scrolls are joined by others.
The children carry *Simchat Torah* flags or miniature scrolls.

Some congregations read Deuteronomy 33:1-17; it is the only time the reading of the Law takes place in the evenings.
During the morning service, another seven-fold procession takes place, followed by reading Deuteronomy 33 and 34. It is customary for all males to be called to the Reading of the Law. Some synagogues allow both men and women to come to the bimah.

During the Kol Hane'arim (Calling up the children) ceremony, the children stand together under a large woolen prayer shawl, while Jacob's blessing is recited:
"God, before whom my fathers Abraham and Isaac did walk, the God which fed me all my life long unto this day... bless the lads [and girls]; and let my name be named on them, and the name of my fathers Abraham and Isaac; and let them grow into a multitude in the midst of the earth." Genesis 48:15-16

The last section of the Pentateuch is reserved for the *Chatan Torah** (Bridegroom of the Law). After the honoured congregant finishes the reading, the congregation says in a loud voice, *"Hazak, hazak, ve'nithazek! (Be strong, be strong and let us be strengthened!)"*
Now a second scroll (Genesis) is taken and the new reading cycle begins.
The person honored to read Genesis 1-2:3 is called the *Chatan Bereshit** (Bridegroom of the beginning). A third person, the *Maftir** is called to read the prophetic reading from Joshua chapter 1. In the past, the two "grooms" had to provide a lavish feast for the whole congregation, but nowadays only wine and light food is served.

In Israel it is customary to hold another, outdoor, *hakkafot* on the night after *Simchat Torah.*

In the synagogues, the Torah is read on Shabbat, most holidays and on the Monday and Thursday mornings. This custom goes back to ancient times when most Jews were farmers or shepherds. On these days they brought their fare to the market. After having sold their produce, the men gathered to read the Torah.

CHAPTER 23

CHANUKAH - THE FEAST OF DEDICATION

Chanukah falls on the 25th of Kislev (December). Because this eight day Festival often coincides with Christmas, it is jokingly called "Chanuchristmas".

When in 175 BC, Antiochus Epiphanes became King of Syria, all citizens had to embrace the Greek religion and culture. In Judea, Sabbath observance was outlawed, *kosher** laws and circumcision forbidden and those found practicing Judaism were killed. By sacrificing pigs on the altar and erecting a statue of Zeus, the Jerusalem Temple was desecrated.
Some Jews complied with Antiochus' decrees. Others became secret believers or chose to become martyrs.
In 167 BC, Mattathias, the village elder and priest of Modi'in, refused to kill the Greek's sacrificial pig and eat its flesh.

When someone offered to perform the rites instead, Mattathias became so enraged that he killed the man. In the ensuing riot, the Greek soldiers were killed by Mattathias, his five sons and some villagers. Together with a group of people who were faithful to the Lord, Mattathias hid in the hills of the Judean Desert. From this area they conducted guerrilla attacks against the Greeks. After the death of Mattathias, Judah became the military leader.
His nickname "Maccabee" is probably derived from the acronym: *"Mi kamocha ba'elim Adonai" – "Who is like you among the gods, oh LORD".*

Even though Jerusalem's Temple was liberated by the Maccabees in 164 BC, it was only in 142 BC that Judean independence was achieved. As sole survivor of the family, Judah's brother Simon became the High Priest and ruler. This was the beginning of the Hasmonean dynasty, which continued until the Roman occupation of Judea in 63 BC.

Chanukah (dedication) refers to the rededication and cleansing of the Second Temple in 164 BC. There was only a one-day supply of pure (*kosher**) olive oil to light the Temple's Menorah* (seven-branched candelabra). The Menorah was lit, and miraculously burned for eight days.

In Jesus' time, *Chanukah* was called the "Feast of Dedication".
"And it was at Jerusalem the feast of the dedication, and it was winter. And Jesus walked in the temple in Solomon's porch." John 10:22-23

The Temple in Jerusalem was the Jewish religious and national symbol.
After its destruction, the religious focus moved to the synagogue. Rabbis switched to the "oil legend" (the miracle that kept the Temple's Menorah burning for eight days). As a visual and hopeful reminder that miracles still happened, people began to light oil lamps in their houses.
Not wanting to irk the Roman occupiers, the Jewish military aspect of the Festival diminished.

Only in the 19th century, with the emergence of the Zionist movement and Jewish nationalism, Chanukah's military aspect re-surfaced. The Jewish people took courage in remembering the strength and courage of the Maccabees.

The festival is observed by kindling lights of a unique candelabrum, the nine-branched Menorah or *Chanukiah**. It has eight branches with an additional raised branch. The extra light is called a *shamash** (attendant or sexton) and used to kindle the other candles. Religious neighborhoods have outdoor *chanukiot* placed along the streets.

On the first night of the Festival public candle

lightning ceremonies are held all over the world. On each night, an additional light is kindled, until all candles burn on the eighth and final night.

After the lighting of the candles it is tradition to sing the hymn *Ma'or Tzur.* The song contains six stanzas. The first and last deal with general themes of divine salvation; the middle four deal with events of persecution in Jewish history, and praise God for survival despite these tragedies:
The exodus from Egypt, the Babylonian captivity, the miracle of the holiday of *Purim*, and the Hasmonean victory over the Greeks.

A popular (non-literal translation) is called "Rock of Ages". Based on the German version by Leopold Stein (1810–1882), it was written by Talmudic linguist Marcus Jastrow and Gustav Gottheil.

Chanukah is the time to eat *sufganiot* (jam-filled donuts) and latkes (potato pancakes). The holiday is celebrated by young and old, but a favourite of families with young children.

The *Sevivon -*

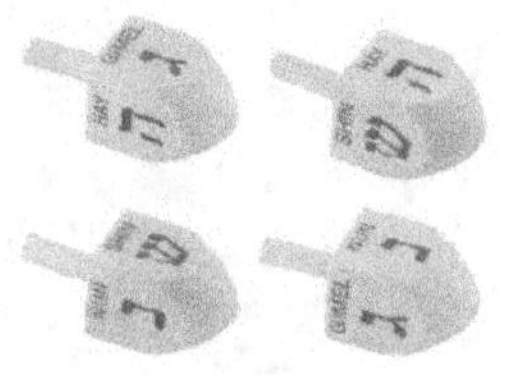

Dreidel (Spinning Top)

A specific *Chanukah* toy is the *sevivon** - spinning top. It is believed that the game originated in India. During the Middle-Ages it was played on Christmas Eve by German Christians. The German Jews replaced the German letters with similar sounding Hebrew ones: *Nun – Gimel – Heh - and Shin*, which is acronym for: *"Nes Gadol Haya Sham"* – a great miracle happened there. In Israel, the *"sham"* (there), is replaced with *"poh"* (here).

CHANUKAH GELT (Money)

The tradition of *Chanukah gelt* (money giving to children during *Chanukah*) originates from a 17th century practice of Polish Jewry to give money to their small children for distribution to their teachers. Later, children were allowed to keep the money for themselves.
In the 18th century, it became custom for poor *yeshiva** students to visit homes of Jewish benefactors dispensing Chanukah money. It is also possible that the custom evolved from Jews in Eastern Europe giving coins to religious teachers as a token of gratitude. (Similar to the custom of tipping service people on Christmas.)

In 1958, the Bank of Israel issued commemorative coins for use as *Chanukah gelt*. That year, the coin bore the image of the menorah that appeared on Maccabean coins 2,000 years earlier.
Children often use chocolate *gelt* to play *dreidel** with. Parents, grandparents or other relatives give older children actual money.

In Chassidic communities, the rabbis continue the practice of distributing small coins to those visiting them during *Chanukah*. Chassidic Jews consider this to be an auspicious blessing from the Rebbe, and a *segulah** for success.

MAOZ TZUR (1st. stanza)

My Refuge, my Rock of salvation!
'Tis pleasant to sing to your praises.
Let our house of prayer be restored.
And there we will offer You our thanks.
When You will have utterly
silenced the loud-mouthed foe.
Then we will celebrate with song and
psalm the altar's dedication.

ROCK OF AGES

*Rock of Ages, let our song,
praise Thy saving power;
Thou, amidst the raging foes,
wast our sheltering tower.
Furious they assailed us,
but Thine arm availed us,
And Thy Word broke
their sword,
when our own strength failed us.*

*Kindling new the holy lamps,
priests, approved in
suffering,
Purified the nation's shrine,
brought to God their offering.
And His courts surrounding,
hear, in joy abounding,
Happy throngs, singing songs
with a mighty sounding.*

*Children of the martyr race,
whether free or fettered,
Wake the echoes of the songs
where ye may be scattered.
Yours the message cheering,
that the time is nearing
Which will see, all men free,
tyrants disappearing.*

"BLI AYIN HA RA"

The *ayin ha ra* - 'evil eye', is the belief that certain individuals have the ability to cause harm by directing their gaze at others. That person inflicts bad luck, sickness or even death. The potential victim therefore devises ways to safeguard himself against this harmful glance by protective charms. This can be a talisman worn around the neck, red and blue colored thread or mirrors to ward off evil. Sephardic and Eastern Jews observe this custom by using blue paint on their door posts, and displaying amulets (like a *Chamsah**) with biblical or Kabbalistic texts. Ashkenazim tie a red ribbon to the new born child. The expression, *"Bli ayin hara"*, means "May no one cast an evil eye - may your positive situation contin-ue."

The Planter's Prayer
Composed by Rabbi Ben-Zion Meir Hai Uzziel, the first Sephardi Chief Rabbi of the State of Israel

Our Father who is in Heaven,
The Builder of Zion and Jerusalem,
Be pleased, O Lord, with Your Land,
And bestow goodness upon it.
From the goodness of Your loving kindness.
Give dew for a blessing, and cause desirable rains To fall in their time.
Satiate the mountains of Israel, and its valleys, And water every plant and tree within them.
As for these saplings that we plant before You today, Deepen their roots and increase their magnificence, That they may blossom and be accepted,

The Fast of *Asarah Betevet*
(The Tenth of Tevet)

The Fast of *Asarah Betevet* (the Tenth of Tevet), after *Chanukah* is a minor fast day (or "low fast"), and therefore only observed from sunrise to sunset. It commemorates the beginning of the siege of Jerusalem by king Nebuchadnezzar II of Babylonia. This event culminated with the destruction of Solomon's Temple (the First Temple) and the conquest of the Kingdom of Judah.

Among the other trees of Israel,
For blessing and for beauty.
Strengthen the hands of all our brethren,
Who labor in the work of the holy soil,
And who cause the wilderness to bloom.
Bless them, O Lord, that they may succeed,
And that the work of their hands be acceptable. Look from Your holy dwelling, from Heaven, And bless Your people Israel.
And the Land which you gave us,
As you swore to your fathers.
Amen.

CHAPTER 24

TU B'SHVAT - THE NEW YEAR OF TREES

"As others have planted for you, so you will plant for your children." Leviticus Rabbah, 28

Tu B'shvat, the 15th of the Hebrew month of Shvat (end of January, beginning of February) is not mentioned in the Bible. However, the

*Mishnah** (part of the Talmud), describes it as the "New Year for trees".
Israel's rainy season is usually over by now, but people still hope for the blessing of the "latter rain". This holiday marks the revival of nature, which is symbolized by the budding of the almond tree.

Leviticus 19 tells us what was expected from the Israelites when they entered the Promised Land: *"When you come to the land and you plant a tree, you shall treat its fruit as forbidden; for 3 years it will be forbidden and not eaten. In the fourth year, all of its fruit shall be sanctified to praise the Lord. In the 5th year you may eat its fruit."* (NIV)

Having a specific date as the New Year for trees also helped with the law of tithing – 1/10th of the farmer's fruit had to be donated to the priests.

Biblical tithes were:

- ♦ ***Orlah*** - refers to a biblical prohibition (Leviticus 19:23) on eating the fruit of trees produced during the first three years after they are planted.
- ♦ ***Neta Reva'i*** - refers to the biblical commandment (Leviticus 19:24) to bring fourth-year fruit crops to Jerusalem as a tithe.
- ♦ ***Ma'aser Sheni*** - was a tithe which was eaten in Jerusalem.
- ♦ ***Ma'aser Ani*** - was a tithe given to the poor (Deuteronomy 14:22-29) that were also calculated by whether the fruit ripened before or after *Tu B'shvat.*

During the Second Temple period it was customary to plant a tree when a child was born - a cedar for a boy (referring to its height and strength), and a cypress (smaller and fragrant) for a girl. When the child married, the wood of the tree was used to make the *chuppah**, the wedding canopy.

Throughout the ages, the diverse Jewish communities in the Diaspora developed all kinds of customs to celebrate this day. In the beginning of the 19th century, when the first Jewish settlers began to redeem Eretz Yisrael, part of their work was to plant trees on the barren and eroded hills.

On *Tu B'shvat,* January 25, 1890, Rabbi Zeev Yavetz and his students set a good example by planting trees in the agricultural colony of Zichron Ya'akov.

The idea to plant trees on *Tu B'shvat,* was in 1908 adopted by the Jewish Teachers Union and later by the Jewish National Fund (*Keren haKayemet leIsrael*), who, amongst other endeavors, began to oversee the forestation of the Land of Israel.

Many of Israel's major institutions have chosen this day for their inauguration ceremonies.

The cornerstone of the Hebrew University of Jerusalem was placed on *Tu B'shvat* 1918, and the first stone of Haifa's Technion was laid on the same day in 1925. The first Jewish parliament of the Jewish sovereign State chose to hold its first Knesset session on T*u B'shvat* 1949.

On T*u b'Shvat* it is customary to eat the types of dried fruit mentioned in Deuteronomy 8:8 (the Seven Species). Some Orthodox Jews make candy from their *Etrog* (one of "Four Species" during Sukkot) and eat it during *Tu B'Shvat.*

The Almond

In January, the gnarled, leafless almond tree begins to bloom; its pinkish white flowers provide ample nectar for the wild bees.

The almond belongs to the peach family. Growing wild in Israel, it can reach a height of 4.5 to 6 meters. The fruit is a drupe – that is, it has a soft, fleshy part around an inner stone that contains the seed. When it ripens, its dry or woody husk splits into two halves. The unripe, greenish fruits are a delicacy to some, but most people prefer the dried stone - the almond we know so well, eaten either salted or ground into a sugary pulp known as marzipan.

Almond buds and blossoms modelled for the Tabernacle's candelabra. Aaron's rod miraculously sprouted leaves and almond blossoms at the same time - God's sign he and his tribe was chosen as priests.
During the seven years of famine, Jacob sent almonds to the Egyptian ruler – a delicacy for them.
In Ecclesiastes, the almond symbolizes old age because the white blossoms are reminiscent of white hair.

Tu B'shvat is sometimes called the Jewish Arbor day. The highlight of the holiday is planting a new sapling in the soil of *Eretz Yisrael*, the Jewish homeland.

Genesis 28:19 mentions Luz. The village probably received its name because the surrounding hills were full of almond trees.

The root from the Hebrew *shaked* (almond) is the word *shoked* (to watch diligently or to wait). In Jeremiah 1:11-12 it is used as wordplay. God asks Jeremiah, Israel's watchman, what he sees, *"I see a rod of an almond (shaked) tree,"* he answers. The Lord replies, *"Thou hast well seen: for I will hasten [watch over] (shoked) my word to perform it."*

In ancient times, dried fruits were either ground into a paste or used for their oil. Almonds were an exclusive cooking ingredient in Roman times. The bitter taste was removed by cooking them in water and the husks were used as fuel.

Ta'anit Esther -Fast of Esther

The Fast of Esther (*Ta'anit Esther*) on the 13th of Adar (before Purim) commemorates the three-day fast observed by the Jewish people in the book of Esther.
Because this is not one of the four public fasts ordained by the Prophets, pregnant women, nursing mothers, and those who are weak are not required to observe it.

CHAPTER 25

PURIM

Purim is the celebration of the deliverance of the Jews from an enemy bent on their destruction. It is celebrated on the 14th and 15th day of Adar (usually in March). Purim is the plural of the Hebrew word *"pur"*, which means lot (used to determine something by chance). It refers to Haman's use of lots to choose the date for his intended destruction of the Jews.

Throughout the book of Esther, *"...the name of God is not there, but His finger certainly is,"* wrote Matthew Henry. *"His providence is obvious – quietly, but sovereignly at work in the lives of men and women."*
Although *Purim* is a minor festival from a religious point of view (it is not mentioned in the Torah as a Feast of the Lord), people celebrate it with fervor.

Until 2 AD, *Purim* was called "the Day of Mordechai", or "day of Protection".
People observed the holiday by reciting the story of the *Megilah** (Scroll) in their homes and by exchanging gifts.

The Talmud describes public readings during the Second Temple period. Priests were instructed to stop their service in the Temple and listen to the recitation. This practice ended with the destruction of the Temple in 70 AD.

With the canonizing of the book of Esther and the appearance of synagogues, public readings in Hebrew and other languages became widespread. Between the end of the 3rd and beginning of the 5th century AD, the reading of the Hebrew Megillah was universally accepted. The liturgy was the same, but the drama, color, merrymaking and pageantry varied from country to country. During the middle Ages, the celebration was enlivened by masquerades, jesters, musicians and actors. Noisemaking and selecting a *Purim* queen or king is traced to 14th Century France. *Purim* plays originated from the 16th century.

In 1615, in Frankfurt, Germany, a local baker pronounced himself the "new Haman" and organized an attack against the Jews of the town. Although they fought back, they were driven out of town, and had to leave their possessions behind. A few months later, the city's ruler realized what injustice had been done. A band welcomed the Jews back to Frankfurt, the baker was killed and his house destroyed.

A plaque described his misdeeds and punishment. From that day on, *Purim* became a special celebration for the Jews in Frankfurt. During the festival they read a special *Megillah* recalling their story.

The walking type of theatre, the *Purim "shpil"* eventually became stage performances. Until World War II, in Germany and Eastern Europe performances took place during the month of Adar. In Western Europe, North America and Israel, the emphasis was more on *Purim* masquerade parties for adults and children.

The book of Esther is usually written on a parchment scroll from a *kosher** animal. The Megillah (scroll) is often illustrated (permitted because the name of God is not mentioned in it). The scroll is read in synagogue on the eve

of *Purim* and the next morning. Each time the name of Haman is mentioned, the people use their *ra'ashan** (greggers) and stamp their feet to drown out Haman's name.

Purim is a feast of gladness, and the only time people are allowed to get drunk – so they no longer remember whether it was Mordechai or Haman who was to be praised or cursed.

During this festival, people send *misloach manot** (gifts to the poor). It is also customary to give money.

In synagogue, just before the reading of the *Megillah*, male congregants often donate coins as a reminder of the custom that every Jew over twenty years old, paid half a shekel for the upkeep of the Temple in Jerusalem.

Because the city of Shusan was a walled city, an extra day was added for the celebrations. This is the reason why a walled city like Jerusalem celebrates *Purim* on the 15th of Adar. Purim is an official school holiday in Israel and the streets are filled with children and adults wearing various costumes, funny hats or wigs.

Oznei Haman or *Haman Tashen* (Haman's ears) are three-cornered cookies which are a favourite *Purim* treat. One of the fillings is poppy-seed, called *"mohn"* in Yiddish, which sounds a bit like "Haman".
Oznei Haman refers to the old European custom of cutting off criminal's ears before they were hanged.

PURIM KATAN - Adar I and II

Because the Jewish year is based on the lunar calendar, an ordinary year has 353 to 355 days. As Jewish holidays are always celebrated on the same lunar calendar day, this means that in certain years Pesach would be either celebrated in summer, autumn or in winter, instead of in spring. To balance out the drift, an extra month was added every three years - Adar I, while the regular month was called Adar II. The "pregnant" or leap year has 383 to 385 days. *Purim* is always celebrated on the 14th (or 15th) of Adar, therefore some communities celebrate a *"Purim Katan"* (a small Purim) when there is a leap year, in addition to the real Purim.

It is believed that Moses was born on the 7th day of Adar I and died on the same day in Adar II.

"So Moses the servant of the Lord died there in the land of Moab, according to the word of the Lord. And he buried him in a valley in the land of Moab, over against Bethpeor: but no man knoweth of his sepulchre unto this day. And Moses was an hundred and twenty years old when he died: his eye was not dim, nor his natural force abated." Deuteronomy 34:5-7

Orthodox Jews fast on this day, and add a special prayer prior to synagogue services. Jewish burial societies often meet on the seventh of Adar.

No one knows the exact place of Moses' death, therefore the IDF has chosen the 7th of Adar to conduct a special memorial service for soldiers whose bodies have not been found or could not be identified. On Mount Herzl's IDF cemetery is a wall bearing the names of 588 fallen Israeli soldiers whose graves are unknown.

CHAPTER 26

MAKING *ALIYAH*
AND THE INGATHERING OF THE EXILES

And when I saw the African Jew
bending over the furnace,
To draw out the ingot of red-hot steel,
And passing it with his tongs
to the immigrant from the Balkans,
I saw a people standing firm
on its foundations.
They are Jews from Tripoli, Turkey,
Sana'a and Lvov,
From Sofia and Yassi, clean-shaven,
heavy-bearded.

Natan Alterman

*Aliyah** is the word that describes the return of the Jewish People from the exile in the Diaspora back to the Land of Israel. The word is derived from the verb "*la'alot*" - "to go up", or "to ascend" in a positive spiritual sense.
A person who makes *aliyah* is called an *oleh* (plural *olim*) meaning "one who goes up". The opposite action, emigration from Israel, is referred to as *yerida* (descent).

According to Jewish tradition, travelling to the Land of Israel is an ascent, both geographically and metaphysically. In early rabbinic times, many Jews lived in Egypt, Babylonia or the Mediterranean basin. They "made an ascent" when visiting Jerusalem, which is 2,700 feet above sea level.

Aliyah, the immigration of Jews to *Eretz Yisrael* (the land of Israel), is an important Jewish cultural concept and a fundamental component of Zionism.

SAYINGS ABOUT *ERETZ YISRAEL*

- A land flowing with milk and honey
- To effect the purchase of a house in the Land of Israel, the deed may even be written on the *Shabbat.*
- Only in the Holy Land can the Jewish spirit develop and be a light for the world.
- God took the measure of all the lands and found that only the Land of Israel was suitable for the Jewish people.
- One who lives in the Land of Israel is considered to worship the One God; one who lives outside the Land of Israel is considered as though he has no God.
- Living in the land of Israel is equal to all the other commandments.
- The first thing to do when you enter the Land of Israel is to cultivate the land.
- The dead of the Land of Israel will be the first to be resurrected [at the end of days].

It is enshrined in Israel's Law of Return, which accords any Jew (deemed as such by *Halacha** and/or Israeli secular law) and eligible non-Jews (a child and a grandchild of a Jew, the spouse of a Jew, the spouse of a child of a Jew and the spouse of a grandchild of a Jew), the legal right to assisted immigration and settlement in Israel, as well as Israeli citizenship.

Many Religious Jews espouse *aliyah* as a return to the Promised Land, and regard it as the fulfilment of God's biblical promise to the descendants of the Hebrew patriarchs Abraham, Isaac and Jacob. Some believe that *Aliyah* is one of the 613 commandments.

In Zionist discourse, *aliyah* (plural *aliyot)* includes both voluntary immigration for ideological, emotional, or practical reasons and, on the other hand, mass flight of persecuted populations of Jews. The vast majority of Israeli Jews today trace their family's recent roots to outside of the country. While many have actively chosen to settle in Israel rather than some other country, many had little or no choice about leaving their previous home countries. While Israel is commonly recognized as "a country of immigrants", it is also, in large measure, a country of refugees.

The very last word of 2 Chronicles 36:23 (Hebrew Bible) is *veya'al,* a verb form derived from the same root as *aliyah*, meaning "let him go up" (to Israel).

Return to the Land of Israel is a recurring theme in Jewish prayers recited three times a day. Also during holiday services on *Pesach* and *Yom Kippur* the prayers conclude with the words *"Next year in Jerusalem."*

Because Jewish lineage can provide a right to Israeli citizenship, *aliyah* has both a secular and a religious significance. In all historical periods during which return to the Land of Israel was possible, Jewish groups and individuals have immigrated back to the Jewish homeland.

For religious Jews, *aliyah* was (and still is) associated with the (first) coming of the Messiah. He was to redeem the Land of Israel from gentile rule and return world Jewry to the land under a Halachic theocracy.

Abraham was the first *'oleh chadash'* when he and his family came to the Land of Canaan in approximately 1800 BC. Jacob and his family went down to Egypt, and centuries later (about 1300 BC.), Moses and Joshua led the Israelites back to Canaan.

After the Babylonian exile, approximately 50,000 Jews returned to Zion following the Cyrus Declaration from 538 BC. Ezra the scribe led the Jewish exiles living in Babylon to their home city of Jerusalem in 459 BC. Others returned throughout the era of the Second Temple.

Throughout the Middle Ages, blood libels, pogroms and persecution led many Jews to the Land of Israel. In the 18th and early 19th centuries, thousands of followers of various Kabbalist and Chassidic rabbis, added considerably to the Jewish populations in Jerusalem, Tiberias, Hebron and Safed.

The messianic dreams of the Vilna Gaon inspired one of the largest pre-Zionist waves of immigration to *Eretz Yisrael.* In 1808, hundreds of the Gaon's disciples, known as *Perushim,* settled in Tiberias and Safed, and later formed the core of the Old Yishuv Jerusalem.

In the first decade of the nineteenth century, thousands of Jews from Persia and Morocco, Yemen and Russia, moved to Israel. Many more were drawn by the expectation of the arrival of the Messiah in the Jewish year 5600 (1840).

Between 1882 and 1903, approximately 35,000 Jews from the Russian Empire (Hoveivei Zion and Bilu movements), and a smaller group from Yemen, settled in what was then Ottoman Palestine. Many established agricultural communities, e.g. Petach Tikvah, Rishon leZion, Rosh Pina and Zichron Ya'akov. Yemenite Jews settled in Silwan, an Arab suburb of Jerusalem, on the slopes of the Mount of Olives.

Between 1904 and 1914, 40,000 (mainly Russian) Jews immigrated to Ottoman Palestine because of pogroms and outbreaks of anti-Semitism. This socialistic, idealistic group established the first kibbutz, Degania, in 1909. They also formed self-defense organizations, such as Hashomer, to counter increasing Arab

WISE WORDS FROM David Ben-Gurion (1886-1973)

- "In Israel, in order to be a realist you must believe in miracles."
- "Ours is a country built more on people than on territory. The Jews will come from everywhere: from France, from Russia, from America, from Yemen... Their faith is their passport."
- "There are eleven million Jews in the world. I don't say that all of them will come here, but I expect several million, and with natural increase I can quite imagine a Jewish state of ten million."
- "Suffering makes a people greater, and we have suffered much. We had a message to give the world, but we were overwhelmed, and the message was cut off in the middle. In time there will be millions of us - becoming stronger and stronger - and we will complete the message."

hostility and to help Jews to protect their communities from Arab bandits.

Eliezer Ben Yehuda revived Hebrew as the national language; Hebrew newspapers and literature were published and political parties and workers organizations were established.

Eliezer Ben Yehuda

After the First World War, between 1919 and 1923, 40,000 (mainly Russian) Jews settled in the country which now had become British Mandate Palestine.

Many pioneers, halutzim, who were trained in agriculture, established self- sustaining economies. Despite British immigration quotas, the Jewish population reached 90,000 by the end of this period. The Jezreel Valley and the Hefer Plain (Hulah Valley) marshes were drained and converted to agricultural use. Additional national institutions arose like the Histadrut (General Labour Federation and the Haganah, the forerunner of the Israel Defence Forces (IDF).

Increasing anti-Semitism in Poland and Hungary led to the arrival of 82,000 Jews between 1924 and 1929. Amongst them were many middle-class families who moved to the growing towns, establishing small businesses and light industry.

The rise of Nazism in Germany brought a new wave of 250,000 immigrants between 1929 and 1939. On this so-called Fifth Aliyah, most people came from Eastern Europe; they also included German professionals, doctors, lawyers and professors. Refugee artists introduced the Bauhaus architecture and founded the Palestine Philharmonic Orchestra. The new Haifa port and its oil refineries added significant industry to the predominantly agricultural economy.

Aliyat Hano'ar (Youth Aliyah) rescued thousands of German Jewish children from the Nazis during the Third Reich. It arranged for their resettlement in British Mandate Palestine in kibbutzim and youth villages that became both home and school.

The organization was founded in 1933 by Recha Freier in Berlin, on the same day that Adolf Hitler took power. Upon arrival in Palestine, the children were welcomed by Henrietta Szold.

In all 5,000 teenagers were brought to Palestine before World War II and educated at Youth Aliyah boarding schools. Others were smuggled out of occupied Europe in the early years of the war, some to Palestine, England and other countries. After the war an additional 15,000 (most of them Holocaust survivors), were brought to Palestine.

Today, Youth Aliyah is a department of the Jewish Agency, which continues to bring young people to Israel from North Africa, Central and Eastern Europe, Latin America, the Soviet Union and Ethiopia.

Tensions between Arabs and Jews continued to rise, which eventually led to the Arab-Israeli conflict. The White Paper of 1939, issued by the pro-Arabic British government, severely restricted Jewish immigration to 75,000 people in five years.

There was no option left but to continue the immigration illegally - the *Aliyah Bet*.

Between 1933–1948, *Ha'apalah* (secondary immigration) was organized by the *Mossad Le'aliyah Bet,* as well as by the Irgun.

Most of the immigrants came by sea, but some overland through Iraq and Syria. Between World War II and Israel's Independence in 1948, Aliyah Bet became the main form of Jewish immigration. After World War II, the illegal immigration escalated when many Holocaust survivors joined the *Aliyah.*

1948–1950 saw the "Ingathering of the Exiles" - the *kibbutz galuyot.*

The American Jewish Joint Distribution Committee (The Joint) had been founded in 1914. Their funds, diplomatic skills, and well-run organization ensured the rescue of Jews on a massive scale. With the birth of the State of Israel in 1948, the Jewish Agency for Israel was mandated as the organization responsible for *aliyah in* the Diaspora.

Soon after its establishment in 1948, the emerging state of Israel found itself lacking in both food and foreign currency. In just three and a half years, the Jewish population of Israel had doubled, increased by nearly 700,000 immigrants. Consequently, the Israeli government instigated measures to control and oversee distribution of necessary resources to ensure equal and ample rations for all Israeli citizens. Austerity did have its advantages – none remained hungry, and shelter was found for all immigrants.

Between 1948 and the early 1970s, around 900,000 Jews from Arab lands left, fled, or were expelled. The entire community of Yemenite Jews (about 49,000) was airlifted to Israel in Operation Magic Carpet.

Operation Ezra and Nehemiah brought 114,000 Iraqi Jews home.
Following the Islamic Revolution, over 30,000 Iranian Jews immigrated to Israel.

The massive airlift known as Operation Moses began to bring Ethiopian Jews to Israel on November 18, 1985 and ended on January 5, 1986. In six week's time, some 6,500–8,000 Ethiopian Jews were flown from Sudan to Israel. An estimated 2,000–4,000 Jews died en route to Sudan or in Sudanese refugee camps. In 1991, Operation Solomon was launched to bring the Beta Israel Jews of Ethiopia.
In one day (May 24), 34 aircraft landed at Addis Ababa and brought 14,325 Jews from Ethiopia to Israel. Ethiopian Jews continue to immigrate to Israel. Today, their number is over 100,000.

Fearing a 'brain-drain' and depletion of their intelligentsia, mass emigration was politically undesirable to the Soviet regime. After the 1967 Six Day War, the state-controlled mass media began anti-Zionist propaganda campaigns.
By the end of 1960s, the majority of Soviet Jews had been assimilated and were non-religious. However, the subsequent Israeli victory in 1973 over Soviet-armed Arab armies stirred up Zionist feelings.
Russian Jewish immigration began en masse in the 1990s when the liberal government of Mikhail Gorbachev opened the borders of the USSR and allowed Jews to leave the country - over one million Soviet Jews immigrated to Israel.

From the year 2000, political and economic instability moved more than 10,000 Argentine Jews to immigrate to Israel. Also affected by the crisis was Uruguay, from which over 500 Jews made *aliyah* in the same period.

In Venezuela, a growth in violent anti-Semitism saw an increasing number of Jews making *aliyah* during the first decade of the 21st century. For the first time in Venezuelan history, Jews began leaving for Israel by the hundreds.

By November 2010, more than half of Venezuela's 20,000-strong Jewish community had left the country.

The Second Intifada in Israel triggered many anti-Semitic incidents in France. Between 2001 and 2005, 11,148 French Jews made Aliyah. Immigration from France is ongoing.

Like Western European olim, North Americans tend to immigrate to Israel more for religious, ideological and political purposes. However, the continuing global financial crisis (which began in 2008), brought many American Jews to Israel for financial reasons. They saw that Israel managed to weather the financial crisis better than the United States and most other countries. In 2009, 4,000 American Jews made aliyah - the largest number in a single year since 1983. Approximately 110,000 North American immigrants now live in Israel and their numbers continue to grow.

The *Nefesh B'Nefesh* organization provides financial assistance, employment services and streamlined governmental procedures for North American and British immigrants.

Since the mid 1990s, there has been a steady stream of South African Jews, American Jews and French Jews who have either made *aliyah,* or purchased property in Israel as an insurance policy for the future.

The immigration of the Bnei Menashe (Sons of Manasseh) Jews from India began in the early 1990's and continues to this day.

On a regular basis, Israeli newspapers publish articles about groups of olim arriving in Israel. It is always a wonderful experience to see or read about a group of new immigrants arriving at Ben Gurion Airport. Proudly waving their Israeli identity card, they are ready to start their new life in Israel.

Some olim receive special attention - especially singles or couples in their eighties or even nineties, who finally decided to 'come home'. The oldest couple ever to make *aliyah* landed in Israel in February 2012. Phillip (95) and Dorothy (93) Grossman from Baltimore were part of a *Nefesh B'Nefesh* group with more than 40 other new immigrants from North America.

Golda Meir had been entrusted by David Ben-Gurion to raise funds for the mass of new immigrants. No one was turned away, and every effort made to find them food and shelter. The theme of her fund-raising was that the money was needed, 'not to win a war, but to maintain life'.
"Sometimes I used to go to Lydda [airport]," *Golda Meir recalled, "and watch the planes from Aden touch down, marveling at the endurance and faith of their exhausted passengers. "Had you ever seen a plane before?" I asked one bearded old man.*

"No," *he answered.* *"But weren't you very frightened of flying?" I persisted.*
"No," he said again, very firmly. "It is all written in the Bible, in Isaiah. "They shall mount up with wings of eagles." *And standing there, on the airfield, he recited the entire passage to me, his face lit with the joy of a fulfilled prophecy - and of the journey's end."*

The Grossmans immediately headed for their new home in Jerusalem. The American-born couple has been married for 71 years. One of their three children already lives in Israel, and a second plans to move to the country this summer.

The oldest person ever to make *aliyah* is a woman from New York who moved to Israel at the age of 102, another Baltimore resident made *aliyah* at the age of 99.

"Absorbing these immigrants would have been beyond the ability of a well-established, prosperous country, let alone one newly born and struggling to defend itself." **Chaim Herzog**

In 1951, Moshe Sharett addressed a mass rally of new immigrants at a housing project near Rishon le-Zion. He gave five separate addresses in Yiddish, Turkish, Arabic, French and Hebrew.

New Olim, proudly showing their Israeli Identity Card

In 2008, Ya'akov Manlun, 97, and his wife Orah, 88, new immigrants from the Bnei Menashe Tribe of India, wed in a lavish ceremony joined by many guests in Kiryat Arba. Ya'akov and Orah had to wait 15 years to receive permission to make *aliyah*. They have nine children (three of which also made *aliyah*), and nearly 70 grandchildren, great-grandchildren, and great-great grandchildren living in Israel and India. The couple had been married for almost 70 years. After concluding their conversion process, they wanted to be remarried according to the Law of Moses.

ALIYAH OVERVIEW

Pre-Zionist *Aliyot* (1700 -1882)

First (Zionist) *Aliyah* (1882-1903)

Second *Aliyah* (1904 - 1923)

Third *Aliyah* (1924 - 1929)

Fourth *Aliyah* (1929 - 1939)

Aliyat ha Noar (Youth Aliyah) 1933 - present)

*Aliyah Bet (*Illegal Immigration) (1933 - 1948)

Early Statehood (1948 - 1950)

Aliyah from Arab and Muslim countries (1948 - early 1970's)

Operation Magic Carpet - Yemenite Jews (1949-1950)

Operation Ezra & Nehemiah - Iraqi Jews (1950-1952)

Moroccan Jewish *Aliyah* (1954-1955)

Aliyah from Iran (1948- present)

Operation Moses - Ethiopian *Aliyah* (1985-1986)

Operation Solomon - Ethiopian Jews (1991)

Aliyah from the Soviet Union and post-Soviet states (1990's)

Aliyah from Argentine and Uruguay (2000 - present)

Venezuelan *Aliya* (2010-present)

French *Aliyah* (2001 - present)

North American *Aliyah* (1983 - present)

South African *Aliyah* (1990 - present)

Bnei Menashe *Aliyah* - India (1990 - present)

CHAPTER 27

SEFER TORAH

According to Jewish law, a *sefer Torah* (plural: *sifrei Torah)* or Torah scroll is a copy of the formal Hebrew text of the Five Books of Moses hand-written on g*evil or klaf* (forms of *kosher* parchment) by using a quill (or other permitted writing utensil) dipped in ink. Producing or commissioning a *sefer Torah* fulfils one of the 613 *Mitzvot.*
The scroll is mainly used in the ritual of Torah reading during Synagogue services. When not used, it is stored in the *Aron Kodesh* (Holy Ark*), usually an ornate curtained-off cabinet or section of the synagogue facing Jerusalem, the direction Jews face when praying.
In Jerusalem, the Ark faces towards the Temple Mount in Jerusalem, where the Temple once stood.

For non-ritual functions, the *Chumash* * (five-part - for the five books of Moses) is used. This is a printed and bound book, often accompanied by commentaries or translations.

Torah reading from a *sefer Torah* is traditionally reserved for Monday and Thursday mornings, as well as for *Shabbat* and Jewish holidays. The presence of a *minyan* * is required for the reading of the Torah to be held in public during the course of the worship services. When the scroll is opened to be read it is laid on a piece of cloth called the *mappah* *. While chanting Torah, the dense text is followed by the aid of a *yad* *, a metal or wooden hand-shaped pointer that protects the scrolls by avoiding unnecessary contact of the skin with the parchment.

When the *sefer Torah* is carried through the synagogue, the members of the congregation may touch the scroll with the edge of their *tallit* and then kiss it as a sign of respect.

Some communities do not robe a *sefer Torah* in a mantle, but use a *tik* (ornamental wooden case protecting the scroll). Sephardi communities call the mantles *vestidos.*

Benediction before reading the Torah

"Praise the Lord who is [alone to be] praised!
Praised be the Lord who is [to be] praised for all eternity.
Blessed are You, Lord our God, King of the universe, who has chosen us from among all peoples and given us His Torah.
Blessed are You, Lord, Giver of the Torah."

Benediction following reading the Torah

"Blessed are You, Lord our God,
King of the universe,
who has given us the Torah of truth
and implanted eternal life within us.
Blessed are You, Lord, Giver of the Torah."

Ketav Stam is the specific Jewish traditional writing with which *sifrei Torah, Tefillin, Mezuzot* and the Five *Megillot* are written. The man who writes them is called a *Sofer Stam.* The writing is done by means of a feather and special ink (*Dyo*) onto special parchment called *Klaf.* Today, some scholars choose to become *sofers*, or trained scribes.

To mark a special occasion or commemoration, communities or individuals commission a *sefer Torah,* which can cost thousands of dollars.

Written entirely in Hebrew, a *sefer Torah* contains 304,805 letters, all of which must be duplicated precisely by a trained *sofer.*
It may take approximately one and a half years to complete a sefer Torah.

An error during transcription may render the scroll *pasul* (invalid). Some errors are inevitable in the course of production. If the mistake involves a word other than the name of God, it may be obliterated from the scroll by scraping the letter(s) off with a sharp object.

If the name of God is written in error, the entire page must be cut from the scroll and a new page added. Written anew from the beginning, the page is then sewn into the scroll to maintain continuity of the document.
The old page is buried in a *genizah*.*

Most modern *sifrei Torah* are written with forty-two lines of text per column (Yemenite Jews use fifty). Very strict rules about the position and appearance of the Hebrew letters are observed, but scribes can use several Hebrew scripts.

The Books of the Torah are:

- Genesis (Bereshit – in the beginning)
- Exodus (Shemot – names)
- Leviticus (Vayyikra - and he called)
- Numbers (Bamidbar – in the desert)
- Deuteronomy (Devarim – words, discourses)

The Hachnasat Sefer Torah Ceremony

Introduction of a new *sefer Torah* into a synagogue is done in a ceremony known as *Hachnasat sefer Torah* (lit. ushering in the Torah scroll). This is often accompanied by celebratory dancing, singing, and a festive meal.

The ancient celebration (around 1000 BCE- 1st Temple era) is described in the Bible where it says that the priests, and even king David, *"danced before the ark [of the Covenant]"* or *"danced before the Lord"*.
Wearing a linen ephod, David danced before the Lord with all his might, while he and all Israel were bringing up the ark of the Lord with shouts and the sound of trumpets. (See 2 Samuel 6:14-15)

The person who commissioned the Torah invites special guests to a celebration. It is a great honor to be given the opportunity to write one of the final letters. Speeches are delivered on the importance of Torah study, supporting Torah, and Torah living.

The *Hachnasat Sefer Torah* ceremony is like a wedding, as acceptance of the Torah is seen as being analogous to a marriage with God. Mount Sinai was the canopy, the Jewish people the bride, the Almighty the groom, and the ring the Torah.
The man honored to carry the new Torah Scroll to the synagogue usually walks under a *chuppah** often made of a *tallit** on four poles.
The happy throng of people, including women and children, dance and sing their way to the synagogue.

A completed sefer Torah is treated with great honor and respect. It is housed in the Ark (*Aron Kodesh* or Hechal**), which in its turn is usually veiled by an embroidered *parochet** (curtain). (See Exodus 26:31-34.)

The scroll itself is often girded with a strip of silk (or *wimpel**) and "robed" with a piece of protective fine fabric, called the "Mantle of the Law".

It is decorated with an ornamental breastplate, scroll-handles (*Ets Hachaim*), and the principal ornament—the "Crown of the Law", which is made to fit over the upper ends of the rollers when the scroll is closed.

Some scrolls have two crowns, one for each upper end. The metalwork is often made of beaten silver, sometimes gilded. The gold and silver ornaments belonging to the scroll are collectively known as *kele kodesh* (sacred vessels), and somewhat resemble the ornaments of the *Cohen Hagadol* (high priest).

The scroll-handles, breastplate and crown often have little bells attached to them. A *yad** may also be hung from the scroll, since the Torah itself should never be touched with the bare finger.

CHAPTER 28

CHANUKAT BAYIT - Jewish Housewarming

> *"What man is there that hath built a new house, and hath not dedicated it? let him go and return to his house, lest he die in the battle, and another man dedicate it."*
> **Deuteronomy 20:5**

This verse commands the dedication of a new home as an official endorsement of its new place and purpose. Jewish life is to be observed in daily conduct, but its two main focal points are the synagogue and the home. Home is seen as the place where some Temple traditions are continued - the *Shabbat* candles, (Temple Menorah), and the dining table (the Altar).

Many religious Jews try to move into a new home on *yom shlishi* (lit. the third day - Tuesday), as this is the only day when God twice said that it was good.

(For this reason, Jewish couples also prefer to get married on a Tuesday.)

Religious Jews will never move into a new home on Shabbat or Jewish holidays. Those that are superstitious, never move on Mondays and Wednesdays, as, according to Kabbalah, the Divine attribute of severity is dominant on these days.

Before moving into a new home, some orthodox Jews have the custom of inviting a group of young children to study Torah in the house. They believe that Torah study of young pure souls has a spiritually purifying effect on the entire area.

Bringing Jewish (religious) books and a charity box into the home before the movers bring in the rest of the boxes, is believed to establish the Jewish flavor of the home.
It is symbolic of the owner's wish that the home will be a haven of study and kindness.

DAYS OF THE JEWISH WEEK

The names are modeled on the seven days mentioned in the Creation story in Genesis: *"... And there was evening and there was morning, one day"*.

Yom Rishon - yom alef - "first day" - Sunday (starting at preceding sunset)
Yom Sheni - yom bet - "second day" - Monday
Yom Shlishi - yom gimel - "third day" - Tuesday
Yom Revi'i - yom dalet - "fourth day" - Wednesday
Yom Chamishi - yom heh - "fifth day" - Thursday
Yom Shishi - yom wav - "sixth day" - Friday
Yom Shabbat - shabbat - "Sabbath day (Rest day)" - Saturday

Many religious Jews leave a certain space or wall free of decoration and furnishing as a remembrance of the destruction of the Temple. Some houses have a so-called 'God's corner', which is exclusively used for prayer and meditation.

In Israel, it has become customary to dedicate a dwelling upon moving in - the *Chanukat Bayit* (home dedication). At this gathering, words of Torah are spoken and family and friends use the occasion to express their blessings and wishes for a fruitful and happy stay in this new home. There are blessings and songs; some people read Psalm 15, which encapsulates the Jewish ideal of human conduct and Psalm 119, where a single acrostic of the word *'bracha'*- blessing, is formed.

Many people use bread, salt and candles to initiate their new home. The bread represents the hope that there will always be enough food; the candles are a symbol of light and joy; and the salt is a reminder of the Temple sacrifices and tears shed.

The assembled guests are greeted by the host with a blessing of welcome,
"We bless all who come in God's name with love and peace to sanctify this place, as we make this house our home."
The host then recites the *shehecheyanu* (recited on many joyous occasions),
"Blessed are You, Lord our God, King of the Universe, who has granted us life, sustained us and enabled us to reach this occasion."

During the housewarming, it has become custom to also eat a new fruit, therefore, the *shehecheyanu* blessing applies both the new home and the new fruit.
If weather permits, everyone gathers outside the front door, and silently meditates upon the blessings they wish for the home.
"Hineh ma tov u'manayim, shevet achim gam Yachad" (See how good it is for brethren to dwell together) is a favourite song for a housewarming party.

An important part of the *Chanukat Bayit* ceremony is the affixation of the *mezuzah** to the house's front and other doors. (With the exception of the bathrooms and toilets.)

The mezuzah is one of many symbols in Judaism, which act as an identifier, a constant reminder of one's obligation towards God as well as an affirmation of the Unity of God.

A mezuzah can be made of wood, metal, stone or ceramic. The parchment within the *mezuzah* is inscribed with the words of Deuteronomy 6:4-9 and 11:13-21. Shaddai or the Hebrew letter *'shin'* is often displayed on the front of the *mezuzah*. *Shaddai'* (Almighty) is one of the names of God, and an abbreviation for 'guardian of the doors of Israel'.

"Guardian of the doors of Israel"

Historically, the *mezuzah* can be dated back to the time when the Jews were slaves in Egypt - all Egyptian houses had a sacred document at their entrance. *Mezuzah* literally means 'doorpost', hence it is placed on the doorpost of the Jewish home, as instructed in Deuteronomy 6:9 and 11:20, *"Inscribe them on the doorposts of your house and on your gates".* Originally, an abbreviated version of the daily prayer known as the Shema was carved into the doorpost of a Jewish home. This practice evolved into a piece of parchment with the 22 lines of the *Shema* written on it and tied to the doorpost. The *Shema* reinforces the Oneness of God. Later, a hollow reed was used to protect the parchment, which eventually developed into a container similar to the ones seen today.

Some people believe that the *mezuzah* serves as an amulet, to protect the home and to bring good luck. In order to accentuate 'protective' mechanism of the *mezuzah*, some ultra-Orthodox Jews add Kabbalistic symbols and inscriptions to the quotations on the parchment. 'Shaddai', which appears on the back of the parchment, is a remaining example of this. The majority however see the *mezuzah* as a reminder not to sin, and to follow God's commandments.

It is considered a religious duty to have a *mezuzah* displayed on the front doorpost of a Jewish home. It is a *mitzvah* (commandment), a righteous act, to make (or donate) a *mezuzah* for someone else's home.

After affixing the *mezuzah*, the host recites, *"Blessed are You Gracious One, our God, sovereign of all worlds, who makes us holy with your mitzvot and commands us to affix the mezuzah. Blessed are You Eternal One, our God, who gives us life and keeps us strong and has brought us to this time."*

The guests are now invited to enter the home for the blessing of the bread, *"Blessed is the One who sustains us with bread."* Everyone now dips a piece of bread in various symbolic condiments: salt (symbolizing a life of holiness) oil (sustenance) or honey (sweetness).

After the blessing of thanksgiving, *"As we bless the Source of Life, so we are blessed,"* the guests are invited to share their personal blessings for the new home.

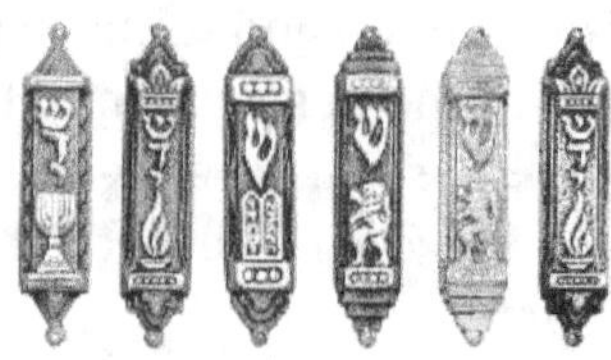

A PRAYER

"Across this threshold may these things never cross: anger and anxiety, hatred and hunger, insult and injury.
May this mezuzah, as we kiss it going in and out, remind all who enter to bring with them only love and laughter, praise and prayer, kindness and comfort. Let the doors of this house be wide open, so all who enter may find shelter and love."

CHAPTER 29

FROM *SHIDDUCH TO CHUPPAH* - MATCHMAKING TO WEDDING

Matchmaking in Biblical Times

The first recorded *shidduch** in the Torah was the match that Eliezer, the servant of the patriarch Abraham, made for his master's son Isaac (Genesis 24). Eliezer received specific instructions to choose a woman from Abraham's own relatives. Throughout Jewish history, arranged marriages were the usual and preferred method to marry off young people. The matchmaking profession was established in the early Middle Ages. The 2% fee was based on the dowry. Often, the shadchan was a Torah scholar who knew most families. Especially in Muslim countries, women were the shadchan. The etymology of the words *shidduch* and shadchan is uncertain. It is believed to be

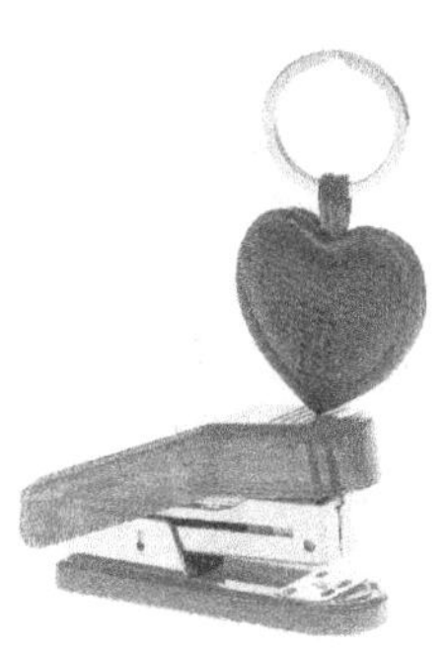

derived from the Aramaic word for "calm". The main purpose of the *shidduch* process is for young people to "settle down" into marriage. In modern Hebrew, a stapler is also called a *shadchan.*

Matchmaking Today

The *shidduch* is a system of matchmaking in which Jewish singles are introduced to one another in Orthodox Jewish communities for the purpose of marriage. In Jewish Law, *shidduch* also refers to what is commonly called engagement; that is, an agreement to marry. A *shidduch* complies with traditional Judaism's outlook on *tzeniut**, modest behavior in relations between men and women, and prevents promiscuity. Orthodox Jews are only allowed to date in order to find a marriage partner.

Both sides (usually the singles themselves, parents, close relatives or friends of the persons involved) make inquiries about the prospective partner, e.g. on his/her character, intelligence, level of learning, financial status, family and health status, appearance and level of religious observance.

A *shidduch* often begins with a recommendation from family members, friends or others who see matchmaking as a *mitzvah**.
A professional *shadchan** (matchmaker), charges a fee for his or her services. Rabbis, who know their congregation well, often act as a matchmaker. However, anyone who makes a *shidduch* is considered a matchmaker. Especially in small Jewish communities, where meeting prospective marriage partners are limited, the *shadchan* gives them access to a broader spectrum of potential candidates.

After the match has been proposed, the prospective partners meet a number of times to find out whether they are right for one another. The number of dates prior to announcing an engagement may vary by community. In some, the dating continues several months. In stricter communities, the couple may decide a few days after originally meeting with each other. Amongst the Chassidim, eighteen is the age when *shadchanim* take notice and *shidduchim* start. In other communities this can be at a later age.

At the request of the couple, the shadchan talks to either side in the beginning stages of the dating to iron out certain issues. The couple is expected to keep the shadchan up-to-date on how the *shidduch* is going.
When the match doesn't work out, the shadchan is contacted and asked to tell the other side that it will not be going ahead. And in case it does work out, of course the couple informs the matchmaker of its success.

Bashow

The prospective partners either date each other (always in a public place, never alone) or in stricter communities they go to a *bashow** (sit in). The young man and his parents visit the young woman in her house to see if the prospective couple is compatible. Both sets of parents talk to each other, and then, when the setting is more relaxed, they go into another room. The youngsters are left in the living room to speak amongst themselves.

Some use this opportunity to actually ask each other pertinent questions, while others just want to see if they like each other, relying more on the information they got from the

shadchan or from other people.

The number of *bashows* prior to announcing an engagement varies. Some have many *bashows* while others have only one, which is typical among the children of Chassidic rabbis.

Bashert

*Bashert** (Yiddish- destiny) is and often used in the context of one's divinely foreordained spouse or soul mate - "*basherte*" (female) or "*basherter*" (male). Some people use the word for fate or destiny of an important event, friendship, or happening.

Modern Jewish singles often say they are looking for their bashert - the person who will complement them perfectly, and whom they will complement perfectly. Since it is considered to have been foreordained by God whom one will marry, one's spouse is considered to be one's bashert by definition, independent of whether the couple's marital life works out well or not.

Considering the prevalence of a number of genetic diseases in both the Ashkenazi and Sephardi communities, several organizations now routinely screen large groups of young people anonymously. When a *shidduch* is suggested, the candidates phone the organization, enter both their PINs, and find out whether their union could result in critically disabled children. Thanks to these organizations, there has been a sharp decrease in the number of children born with Tay-Sachs disease and other genetic disorders.

A JEWISH WEDDING

"For as a young man marrieth a virgin, so shall thy sons marry thee: and as the bride-groom rejoiceth over the bride, so shall thy God rejoice over thee." Isaiah 62:5

A Jewish Wedding in Ancient Times

In Biblical times, marriage was more a matter of business than of pleasure. Through a negotiated covenant, two households (preferably family) were brought together and goods and services were exchanged over a period of time. The father of the household was responsible for choosing who was eligible to marry. It was usually a friend of the bridegroom, or a trusted servant, who began negotiations with the bride's father, or another representative.

The marriage contract was only established after a series of negotiations. The *mohar* (bride price) and *zebed* (dowry) had to be agreed upon. The bride-price had to compensate the bride's family for the loss of the woman's work, while a dowry was the capital the bride's family invested in the household of her husband.

It transferred the bride's share of her father's inheritance to the children which she and her husband hoped to have. Part of the dowry could come in the form of a circlet of coins that were attached to the woman's head dress. Men usually married around the age of twenty; for girls it was often around the age of fifteen, sometimes even younger.

During the betrothal ceremony, the bride lifted a cup of wine in her right hand. (The right hand was a place of power.) By drinking from the cup, she sealed the betrothal.
A written marriage contract was drawn up, which stated that the *chatan** (lit. one who enters a covenant, the bridegroom) would provide and care for his bride in every way. Signed before two witnesses, the contract was then given to the bride's father.
The couple now both drank from the so-called "shared cup", the cup of the *Brit* (Covenant). The betrothal secured, i.e. sealed, the two were now officially married.

The betrothal (engagement) was a private agreement, in which the father of the bride stated, *"You shall now be my son in law."* (See 1 Samuel 18:21).
The bridegroom then brought out gifts for the bride and her family.

The contract was so binding that that it could not be broken without an official divorce. The couple was considered bound together from the period they entered the betrothal contract until the wedding day. Even though they now were officially 'married', the couple could not yet live together or have sexual intercourse. From this day onwards, the girl had to wear a veil outside the home, even when meeting her betrothed.
Before departing to his father's house, the bridegroom often made a pledge, affirming he would return for his bride. Usually, it would take a year before the wedding took place.

During this time, the bridegroom built the bridal chamber, and the bride prepared her wedding trousseau. She did not know the exact time her bridegroom would come. Only when the father of the groom decided the wedding chamber was ready, would he allow his son to fetch his bride.

Weddings usually took place in spring (when the rainy season was over), before the grain harvesting or in autumn, after the harvest of the fruit crops.
Sometimes, a bridegroom and his friends would come in the middle of the night to snatch away his bride. To let them know they were coming, (so the bride would be ready), they would blow the *shofar**.

A Hebrew bride is called a *kallah** (meaning 'complete' or 'enclosed one').
Before the wedding, she underwent a ritual immersion (*mikvah/mikveh**) to symbolize her turning aside from all the former things and starting a new life with her husband. Her 'companions' braided her hair and helped her put on a brightly colored dress. Then she was adorned with all the jewels she possessed.

On her veil was an ornamental headdress, suggesting the appearance of a queen, while the groom also wore a diadem on his head.

Sometimes bride and groom were carried on a litter, like a king and queen.
During the bridal procession, the bride was heavily veiled. She would remain so until the marriage was consummated on the first night. Another custom was for the bridegroom to remove the veil, lay it upon his shoulder and declare, *"The government shall be upon his shoulder."*
This indicated that the bride had passed from the authority of her father to that of her husband.

Lighted by torchbearers and accompanied by tambourines and musicians, the procession moved towards the house of the bridegroom. Wise companions of the bride made sure they had enough oil in their lamps to accompany their friend to the wedding feast.

The wedding feast began upon the arrival of the couple at the house of the bridegroom. The marriage covenant was ratified when he spread his cloak over this bride and called her isha (wife). The couple was blessed with,
"Our sister, may you increase to thousands upon thousands; may your offspring possess the gates of their enemies." Genesis 24:60 (NIV)
Wealthy families provided wedding clothes for the guests.
The marriage feast was a time of rejoicing, music making, dancing, singing and asking of riddles. The wine flowed, and there was plenty of food.

Under the eyes of the wedding guests, the couple retired to the wedding chamber to consummate their wedding.
To become *echad* (one flesh) is also called *kiddushim/kiddushin* (sanctification or ratification). The ancient name is *yichud** ("the knowing.")

The bride's family showed the blood-stained bed coverings to the guests, who were now witnesses that the marriage had been consummated. Proof of the bride's virginity was her insurance policy. In case of doubt, her in-laws could refuse to pay the bride-price.

A marriage only became legal when both the dowry and the bride price were paid during the seven days of wedding celebrations.
The transfer had to be officially witnessed by the village or city elders and other wedding guests.
The bridal chamber, in which the couple consummated their marriage began to be called the *chuppah** in Talmudic times.
The legally married couple would first spend an hour together in an ordinary room, after which the bride entered the chuppah. Only after gaining her permission, the groom would join her. Joel 2:16 and Psalm 19:5 speak about the 'bridal chamber' and a 'pavilion'.

In Talmudic times, Sunday and Wednesday were suitable wedding days because the court met on Monday and Thursday. Any contention as to virginity of the bride could be lodged immediately after the wedding night.

Some communities preferred to have weddings on a *Rosh Chodesh** (unless it coincided with *Shabbat* or other prohibited days). The waxing moon was considered a symbol of growth and fertility. Because travelling, working and making a new agreement were prohibited on *Shabbat,* weddings could not take place on that day. *Shabbat* was always a day of joy, and each opportunity for joy and celebration was to be observed individually, and not combined with another. Two members of the same family would not even think of marrying on the same day.

A Jewish Wedding Today

In modern times, *yom shlishi,* the third day of the week (Tuesday) continues to be a favourite day for a wedding, because in Genesis 1:10-12 it says twice, *"... and God saw that it was good."*

The two events (betrothal and marriage) became one single ceremony during the Middle Ages (around the 16th century). Today, a Jewish wedding has two distinct stages or *kiddushim* (sanctification or dedication) which are the *erusin** (betrothal) and *nissuin** (marriage).
While in ancient times, there could be a year between these two events, today they are often combined into one ceremony.
Wedding customs and traditions may vary amongst Sephardic and Ashkenazi Jews as well as amongst those of varying levels of religious observance.
In this chapter we describe the customs of an Ashkenazi religious wedding.
The *chatan** (groom) and *kallah** (bride) are likened to a King and Queen and therefore to be treated with great honor and fanfare prior to, during the wedding and in the week following their union.

A recent custom is the *Shabbat Kallah* which takes place on the Shabbat before the wedding. Women friends celebrate the bride, bring her joy, make her laugh, and help her overcome possible last minute jitters.

The *mikvah/mikveh** (ritual bath) is an essential part of the Jewish laws of family purity. During the engagement period, it is customary for the couple to study these laws with a teacher. In order to purify herself spiritually, a bride immerses herself in the *mikveh* within the final 4 days before the wedding. Usually, the groom also pays a visit to the ritual bath for the same reason.

Bride and groom are not allowed to see each other in the week before the wedding. The community believes this will increase the joy of seeing each other again on their wedding day.

A *shomer/shomeret** (lit. guard) has the role of the best man/maid of honor. They act as go-betweens for the couple during the week that they cannot see each other.
On the wedding day, they make sure the bride and groom arrive to the wedding safely and as stress-free as possible.

As the couple are about to start a new life together, the wedding day is considered to be a personal *Yom Kippur* for the bride and groom. Observant Jews even add the *Yom Kippur* confessional to their private afternoon prayers. This is also the reason why many couples refrain from eating and drinking on their wedding day, unless they feel weak or have an illness.

*Tena'im** are betrothal documents similar to an engagement contract, agreed upon and signed by two representatives - one of the groom and one of the bride. Because breaking a betrothal is considered to be a grave breach of honor, most couples arrange for the *Tena'im* to be signed just before the wedding.

*Kabbalat Panim** (lit. Greeting of Faces) is the opening reception of the wedding. During the *Kabbalat Panim* the bride and groom truly become like a King and Queen. Sitting on a throne-like chair and surrounded by the women of her family, the bride greets female guests. In her role as Queen for the day, she often blesses her friends.

Male guests come to greet the groom at his *Tisch* (Yiddish - table). They sometimes share a *l'chaim* (toast) in his honor.
During this reception, the *tena'im* is concluded and signed by two witnesses.

After reading the tena'im aloud, the "breaking of the plate" ceremony takes place.
By smashing a ceramic plate together, mothers of the bride and groom symbolize the seriousness of the commitment between their families - Just as breaking the plate is final, so too is the engagement.

Now legally engaged, the couple can be contractually married. Two witnesses sign the ketubah, spelling out the husband's obligation to his wife; from sustaining her with basic necessities to honoring and cherishing her. The document also describes how the husband must support his wife during their lives together, and, God forbid, in the event of death or divorce. This legally binding agreement is often written as an illuminated manuscript. Many people have it framed and displayed in their home.

According to Orthodox Jewish law, a *ketubah* is considered binding once it has been signed by the two witnesses. The signatures of the bride, groom and wedding officiant are a modern addition to the ketubah, and are not required to make it binding. This is because, in ancient times, the groom would read the Aramaic document aloud, and two adult males - unrelated to bride or groom - would sign the document, attesting to the groom's verbal agreement to the ketubah contract.
Even after the signing of the contract, the couple is only considered officially married after the chuppah ceremony.

The custom of the bride wearing a veil goes back to the Biblical matriarch, Rebecca, who veiled herself upon seeing her future husband, Isaac (Genesis. 24:65). The *bedecken* (Yiddish 'covering') is the veiling of the bride by the groom. With great fanfare, dancing and singing, the guests escort the groom to the bride.

He carefully looks at his bride to confirm that this is his intended bride, and that he will not be deceived as was Jacob when Leah was substituted for Rachel (Genesis 29:23). The groom then lowers the veil over the bride's face. The father of the bride then gives a special blessing to his daughter.

Surrounded by his enthusiastic friends, the groom is escorted out of the room to prepare for the *chuppah.*

In ancient times, the *chuppah* had been the bridal chamber or a pavilion. Over time, it lost its original meaning and was replaced with various other customs. The wedding ceremony was performed under a canopy, which was called the *chuppah*. The bride's entry under the canopy (which resembled a room) was seen as a symbol of the consummation of the marriage.

Today, the *chuppah* (lit. covering) is a canopy under which a bride and groom stand during their wedding ceremony.

It consists of a cloth or sheet, (sometimes *tallit*), stretched or supported over four poles. Sometimes friends of the groom hold up the poles. A *chuppah* symbolizes the home that the couple will build together. This "home", initially lacking furniture, serves as a reminder that the basis of a Jewish home is the people within it, not the possessions. In a spiritual sense, the covering of the chuppah represents the presence of God over the covenant of marriage.

Lacking walls, this encourages the couple to follow in the ways of Abraham and Sarah, whose tent was always open to guests.
The groom enters the *chuppah* first to represent his ownership of the home on behalf of the couple. When the bride then enters the chuppah it is as though the groom provides her with shelter or clothing - he publicly demonstrates his new responsibilities toward her.

In many communities, the groom is led under the *chuppah* by the two fathers and the bride by the two mothers, known as *unterfirers* (lit. ones who lead under).
The groom is welcomed with the song *"Baruch Ha Ba!"* (Blessed is he who comes).
An Ashkenazi groom will often wear a simple white robe, known as a *kittel**. Being both dressed in white is symbolic of purity and creates the imagery of angels.
Entering last, the bride meets her groom and circles her husband-to-be three or seven times. This may derive from Jeremiah 31:22, *"A woman shall surround a man"*.
The three circuits may represent the three virtues of marriage: righteousness, justice and loving kindness (see Hosea 2:21). Seven is the number of perfection or completeness.
It also symbolizes the seven days of creation, and the fact that the couple is about to create their own "new world" together. Seven times it is written in the Torah, *"...and when a man takes a wife."*
Joshua circled the city of Jericho seven times. As two people enter into marriage, there may be 'walls' between them, which have to fall. After the seventh circling of the groom the bride stands to his right under the chuppah.

The wedding ceremony begins with a *kiddush** (blessing of wine). The rabbi recites a blessing over a cup of wine and a second blessing of sanctification over the marriage. The bride and the groom then drink from the cup.

Placing a solid gold band on the right index finger of the bride, (the finger most visible to the witnesses) the groom declares: *"Behold, you are consecrated unto me with this ring according to the laws of Moses and Israel."*

The ring validates the marriage contract and consecrates it. Jewish wedding rings must be made of solid uninterrupted gold, silver or platinum with no precious stones or holes breaking the circle. The continuity of the ring represents the hope for an everlasting marriage.

Sometimes, the bride also presents a ring to the groom, quoting from the Song of Songs: *"Ani l'dodi, ve dodi li "* (I am my beloved's and my beloved is mine), which may also be inscribed on the ring itself. In order to avoid conflicts with Jewish Law, this ring is sometimes presented outside the chuppah.
The two blessings (over the wine and the marriage) and the giving of the ring completes the betrothal ceremony.

To make a distinction between the betrothal and the wedding ceremony, the *ketubah* is read aloud, after which the groom hands the document to the bride.
Now officially husband and wife, the second half of the ceremony commences with a custom called *Nissuin* (uplifting).

A second cup of wine is filled during which the *Sheva Brachot** (seven blessings) are recited. These special blessings are recited both under the chuppah and at the end of the festive meal that follows the ceremony. It is a great honor to be called up to recite one of the seven blessings.

- The First Blessing, recited over a cup of wine, is a sign of rejoicing.
- The Second Blessing thanks God for creating the world and honors the wedding guests.

- The Third and Fourth Blessings acknowledge God's physical and spiritual creation of humankind.
- The Fifth Blessing is a prayer for the restoration of Jerusalem and the rebuilding of the Holy Temple.
- The Sixth Blessing expresses the hope that the bride and groom grow in their love for each other.
- The Seventh Blessing is a prayer that the time of the Messiah will come to redeem the Jewish people from exile so that peace and tranquillity will reign over the world.

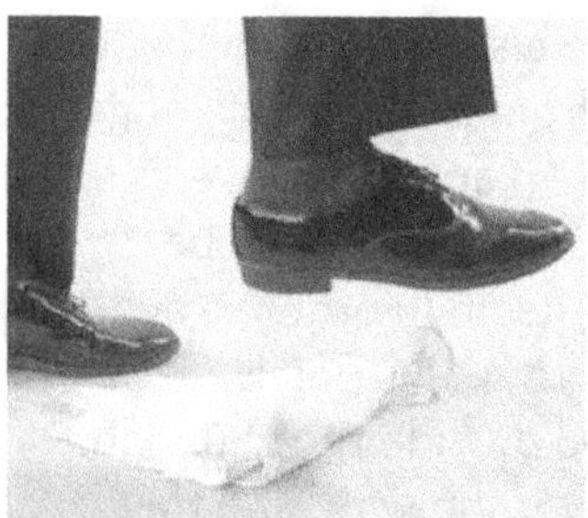

The bride and groom now drink from the second cup of wine, after which the groom smashes a glass with his foot.

All the guests then shout *"Mazal Tov !"* (congratulations and good luck).

Some see the breaking of the glass as a symbolic reminder of the destruction of the temple in Jerusalem; others interpret is as a symbol of the fragility of a relationship. During this part of the ceremony *"If I forget thee O' Jerusalem..."* (Psalm 137:5) is often recited or sung.

The bride and groom, now husband and wife, are escorted to a private room where they spend 10-20 minutes in each other's company.

They are not to be disturbed in the *Yichud** (togetherness, seclusion) room.

When they return, it is time to have dinner with music and dancing.

At Orthodox Jewish weddings it is considered a mitzvah (good deed) to entertain the bride and groom. Friends of the bridegroom do acrobatics or wear funny costumes to entertain the couple.

This is called *Simchat Chatan ve'Kallah*. During this "gladdening of the groom and bride", guests dance around her, often using a *"shtick"*—silly items such as signs, banners, costumes, confetti, and jump ropes made of table napkins.

In separate rooms (or one hall divided by a curtain) male and female wedding guests enjoy *"Simcha* dancing". While singing *"Hava Nagillah"*, guests dance the *Horah*, a well known Jewish circle dance.

The highlight of the wedding is when family members and honored rabbis are invited for the *Mitzvah Tanz*. (See next page.)

Birkat Hamazon (Grace after Meals, *benshen* in Yiddish) is recited at the end of the festive meal to thank God for the food and sustenance that has been enjoyed. A second recitation of the *Sheva Brachot* (Seven Blessings) repeats the blessings that were said under the *chuppah*.

A formal *Birkat Hamazon* has two cups of wine. The first cup is held by the one who leads the prayers. The second cup is passed around amongst those who are honored to recite six of the seven blessings. The last blessing is over the wine.

Then, the two glasses of wine are poured together into a third, symbolizing the creation of a new life together, and drunk by the bride and groom.

MITZVAH TANZ

Before this special event, the bride and a few women, usually her relatives and some important *rebbetzins* (rabbi's wives) are brought to the men's section. Sometimes the *mechitza* is moved aside entirely and the women face the men sitting on the other side of the room.

This wedding dance is different than any other dance. The (often veiled) bride stands like a luminous white vision amongst the male wedding guests. She holds one end of a *gartel**, while the other end is held by the person designated to dance with her. The order of the dancers is significant: the uncles and brothers, the father-in-law, who gives way to the dance with her father, who then gives ultimate precedence to the groom - the other half of her soul. The *Mitzvah Tanz* is a dance of the *Shekinah* and the Jewish People, who are found. Wedding guests enjoy watching this dance because their own souls are dancing. Together as one, they experience the deep thankfulness of bride and groom coming home. The *Mitzvah Tanz* is like an answer that speaks without words. It moves without hardly moving. It soars with the gentle tapping of the feet. It speaks of the flight of souls, the bird soaring and then flying low, the earth and the Heavens. It is a dance of one, and not of two - a dance of One. Excerpt from "Jewish Magazine" article by Varda Branfman.

In the week following the wedding, it is customary for friends and relatives to host festive meals in honor of the new couple.

This is called the week of *Sheva Brachot* because the seven blessings are repeated after the 'Grace after Meals' at each of these festive meals.

On the *Shabbat* after the wedding, it is customary for the groom to be invited for an *Aufruf* * to recite a blessing over the Torah. While the congregation sings *"Siman tov u'mazal tov"* the groom is pelted with candy -

a fun way to wish him a sweet new life. This custom is based on a Talmudic source that records that King Solomon built a special gate for bridegrooms who would pass through it on *Shabbat* to be greeted and blessed by family and friends. After the destruction of the Second Temple, the custom was moved to the synagogue.

It is customary for wedding guests to bring an envelope with money, to help pay for the dinner expenses and the renting of the wedding hall. Unfortunately, the noise of the music band is often too loud to be able to have a conversation with fellow guests at the table. However, being invited to a religious wedding is an unforgettable experience.

CHAPTER 30

BIRTHDAY - *BRIT MILAH AND PIDIYON HABEN*

The only Biblical reference to a birthday was that of Pharaoh. (Genesis 40:20).
The *Mishnah* only refers to birthday celebrations of pagan rulers but is silent on birthday celebrations amongst Jews.
In ancient times Jews saw a birthday as a gloomy reminder that life is drawing closer to its end; a day for solemn reflection and repentance rather than festivity.

According to the Jewish sages, on a person's birthday his "*mazal*" is dominant. The Talmud explains that the miracle of Purim is largely credited to the fact that Moses' birthday occurred during the month of Adar! *Rosh Hashanah* is seen as the birthday of Adam, while *Pesach* is the collective birthday of the Jewish Nation (see Ezekiel 16).

Today, a Jewish birthday is a day to express gratitude to God for being brought into this world. The person has a mission: to illuminate it with the radiance of Torah and *Mitzvot.* Being compared to a personal *Rosh Hashanah,* one is expected to use the gained life experience to make the following year even more productive and fruitful.

Many Israelis celebrate their birthdays, even though this practice was copied from non-Jews. A birthday cake always has an extra candle- one for the new year.
A customary birthday blessing is, *"May you live to be 120"* - the age at which Moses died (See Deuteronomy 34: 7).
Psalms 90:10 suggest that it is good for one who has reached the age of 70 or 80 years to give special thanks to God for having spared him.

According to Ethics of the Fathers 5.21,

"The age of five for the study of the Bible;
then ten for the study of the Mishnah;
13 for the commandments;
15 for the study of Talmud;
18 for marriage;
20 for earning a living;
30 for power;
40 for understanding;
50 for giving advice;
60 for old age, seventy for grey hairs;
80 for special strength,
90 for bowed back;
100 - it is as if he had died and passed away."

BRIT MILAH - CIRCUMCISION

"This is my covenant, which ye shall keep, between me and you and thy seed after thee; Every man child among you shall be circumcised. And ye shall circumcise the flesh of your foreskin; and it shall be a to-ken of the covenant betwixt me and you. And he that is eight days old shall be cir-cumcised among you, every man child in your generations, he that is born in the house, or bought with money of any stranger, which is not of thy seed. He that is born in thy house, and he that is bought with thy money, must needs be circum-cised: and my covenant shall be in your flesh for an everlasting covenant. And the uncircumcised man child whose flesh of his foreskin is not circumcised, that soul shall be cut off from his people; he hath broken my covenant." Genesis 17:10-14

Circumcision in Ancient Times

Children, and especially boys, were (and still are) seen as a blessing of the Lord. Daughters would leave the family upon their marriage, but sons remained. They were the old age assurance of their parents.

In Old Testament times, a child of either sex was named on the day it was born. In New Testament times, a son received his name at the time of his circumcision.

The removal of the male foreskin by cutting became standard practice when the Israelites settled in Canaan. Using a flint knife, the father would circumcise his son on the eighth day. (Leviticus 12:3). This was the outward sign of the covenant between God and Israel. (Genesis 17:10-14).

Only those who had been circumcised were accepted into the community of people that were separated from their heathen neighbors. No uncircumcised foreigner could share in the Passover. Heads of households also circumcised their slaves, whether they were native or foreign.

Brit Milah Today

After the birth of a child, the father is given the honor of an *aliyah** in synagogue.

The congregation recites a blessing for the health of the mother and the child. A girl is named during this *aliyah,* but a boy only receives his name during the *Brit Milah.*

Of all of the commandments in Judaism, the *brit milah* (lit. Covenant of Circumcision) is probably the one most universally observed. It is commonly referred to as a *bris* (Yiddish, covenant) or brit. In Israel, even secular Jews observe these laws. The commandment to circumcise is given in Genesis 17:10-14 and Leviticus 12:3. The covenant was originally made with Abraham and became the first commandment specific to the Jews.

The *brit milah* is performed on eight day-old male infants by a *mohel**. Scientists have proved that an infant's blood clotting mechanism stabilizes on the eighth day after birth. Although some cultures have a practice of removing all or part of the woman's clitoris, often erroneously referred to as "female circumcision," that ritual has never been a part of Judaism.

Most *brit milah* are performed in a synagogue, but can also be done at home or another location. Traditionally, a brit is performed in the morning, but can take place any time during daylight hours and even on *Shabbat.*

In case the baby is born prematurely or when it has serious medical problems, the *brit milah* will be postponed until the doctors and *mohel* deem the child strong enough.

A *mohel* is a pious, observant Jew educated in the relevant Jewish law and in surgical techniques. Circumcision performed by a surgeon does not qualify as a valid *brit milah,* regardless of whether a rabbi says a blessing over it. The reason is that the removal of the foreskin is seen as a religious ritual that must be performed by someone religiously qualified.

The person carrying the baby from the mother to the father is called a *kvatter or kvatterin* (female). This honor is usually given to a couple without children, as a merit or *segulah** (brings good luck) that they should have children of their own.

The term may also be derived from "*gevatter*", an archaic German word for godfather, or a Yiddish combination of the words *kavod* (honor) and *tor* (Yiddish for door). In other words, "The person honored by bringing the baby".

The father then carries his son to the *sandek** (godfather), or person honored to hold the child during the circumcision.

The *sandek*, usually a grandparent or the family's rabbi, often sits in an ornate chair. This special seat is traditionally set aside for Elijah, who is said to preside over all circumcisions. Different blessings are recited (including one over wine), and a drop of wine is placed in the child's mouth.

Now is the time to give the child its formal Hebrew name. These names are mostly used in Jewish rituals, like calling someone to the Torah for an *aliyah**, or in the *ketubah** (marriage contract). The standard form of a Hebrew name is e.g. *Moshe ben Joseph* (Moshe the son of Joseph). A girl is named e.g. *Rivka bat Joseph* (Rivkah, daughter of Joseph. If the child is a Cohen (from the priestly line) they add "ha Cohen". If the child is of the tribe of Levi, "Ha Levi" is added. Amongst Ashkenazim it is customary to name a child after a recently deceased relative. This is done to honor the dead relative, and because they believe it brings bad luck to name a child after a living relative. Sephardic Jews usually do not name a child after a parent or living relative.

After the ceremony, a *seudat mitzvah* (celebratory meal) takes place. Following the *birkat hamazon* (blessing after the meal), special prayers are recited asking God to bless the parents, the *sandek* and the *mohel*. They also ask God to send the Messiah and Elijah the prophet, known as "The Righteous Cohen". Their coming will fulfil God's covenant to re-establish the throne of King David.

Pidyon Haben
Redemption of the First Born

Custom in Ancient Times
According to Jewish Law, a firstborn son had to be redeemed when he was 30 days old. When the days of the mother's purification were over, the parents took the child to the Temple. By paying the priest five shekels of silver the child was 'redeemed'. (See Numbers 3:47-48). Eventually, the five shekel redemption fee became a religious tax.

Custom Today
Most ultra-orthodox and many observant Jews continue to observe the ritual of *pidyon haben*. The ceremony, mentioned in Numbers 18:15-16, only applies to boys that were born by way of a natural birth. If the first pregnancy ended after more than 40 days, the next son does not have to be redeemed. Neither does the redemption of the firstborn apply to members of the tribe of Levi, or children born to a daughter of a member of the tribe of Levi. While a *brit milah* can take place on a *Shabbat*, the ritual of *pidyon haben* cannot, because it involves the exchange of money.

In the traditional ceremony, which takes place before a *minyan**, the father brings the child to the Cohen. The baby is sometimes presented on a silver tray, surrounded by jewelry lent for the occasion by female guests.

Either by reciting a formula or responding to ritual questions, the father states that this is the Israelite mother's firstborn son and he has come to redeem him as commanded in the Torah.

The Cohen (from the priestly line of Aaron) asks the father which he would rather have, the child or the five silver shekels which he must pay. After responding that he prefers the child to the money, the father then recites a blessing and hands over five silver coins (or an equivalent amount of total silver) to the Cohen.

Pidyon haben coin from the Middle Ages

Only a rabbi who is also a Cohen can validate the redemption. While holding the coins over the baby, the Cohen declares that the redemption price is received and accepted in place of the firstborn child. He then blesses the baby and returns him to the custody of his family.

This special event is followed by a festive meal. Sometimes, guests are given cloves of garlic and cubes of sugar to take home. It is believed that by using these items, those who eat them extend the *mitzvah** of participating in the ceremony.

WIMPEL CEREMONY

The *wimpel** (Yiddish/German, "cloth", (derived from Old German, *bewimfen,* meaning "to cover up" or "conceal") is a long, linen sash that German Jews used as a cover for the Sefer Torah. It was made from the cloth used to swaddle a baby boy at his *brit milah*. This custom united the Jewish community with the individual's own life cycle.

In the Middle Ages, most Torah scrolls were wrapped with a *mappah** (cloth). It was considered a *mitzvah* and honor to donate such a *mappah* to the congregation. Often, a groom would donate one on the eve of his wedding. Because most of the coverings were made from old clothing, some rabbis disapproved - they thought it was disrespectful for the Torah.

During the Middle Ages, it was customary to wrap a baby's legs after the circumcision to prevent him from moving around and knocking the bandages out of place. One day, the *mohel* forgot to bring along the cloth for the baby's legs. Believing this was a life-threatening situation, the rabbi gave permission for the *mohel* to use a spare *mappah* from one of the synagogue's Torah scrolls. The baby's parents were asked to wash the cloth before returning it to the synagogue.

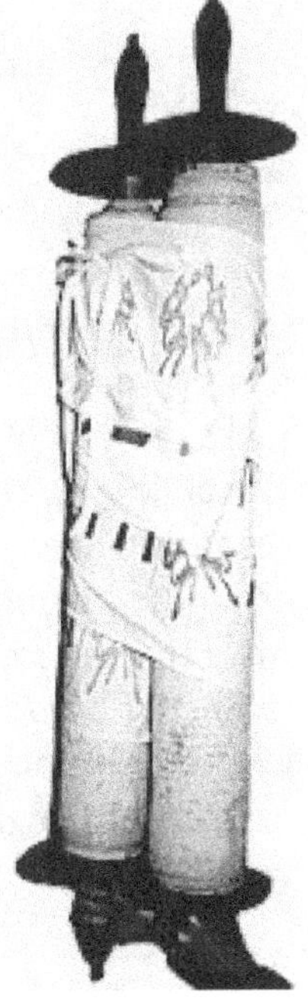

Another version is that the *mohel* used to place a long swath of white cloth (the *wimpel)* under the pillow on which the baby lay for his circumcision.

After the ceremony, the wimple was either painted or embroidered. It had the child's name, date of birth, and the Hebrew blessing, *"Just like he entered the [covenant of] circumcision, so too he should [the covenant of] Torah, marriage, and good deeds."*
Some mothers did the artwork themselves; others retained the services of *"wimpel professionals"*.

Because both the Torah and circumcision relate to covenants that the Jewish people have with God, the cloth used at a circumcision was considered 'holy'. It therefore became custom to donate these *wimpels as mappot* to the synagogue.

Foto: Mercy Gaynoor

Today, many synagogues still have a '*wimpel* ceremony' when a boy turns three (and is deemed toilet trained). This is also the age that a religious boy begins to learn Torah. On *Shabbat* morning, father and son are called up after the first reading of the Torah. With the help of his father, the child then wraps the *wimpel* many times around the Torah scroll and tucks the end of the cloth into the folds. In a symbolic way, the child wraps his individual responsibilities to God and His commandments around his communal responsibilities.
After the service, everyone is invited to join the family for a *kiddush** and small party. The joyous occasion is meant to instill a love and enthusiasm for *shul* (synagogue) and Judaism within the child.

In Germany, once a Jewish boy is free from diapers, he is brought to the synagogue. When the men carry the Torah below *ezrat nashim** (place where the women sit in Synagogue, usually the balcony), the mother throws the *wimpel* on the Torah. The dedicated *wimpel* symbolizes the fact that the child is now 'pure' and able to take part in the service and to learn Torah.

Often, the synagogue receives many more *wimpels* than it has Torah scrolls. These are then stored in a drawer in the Ark*. It is customary to place the boy's *wimpel* on the Torah during his *Bar Mitzvah, an Aufru*f or other important family events. Some *wimpels* are even used as a decorative banner on the groom's *chuppah.*

In many synagogues around the world, the '*wimpel* ceremony' continues to be an integrated and joyous part of Jewish life cycle events.

A *wimpel* is created from the *brith mila's* swaddling cloth. After it has been washed, the cloth is cut into strips and sewn into a sash measuring six or seven inches wide and ten or twelve feet long. Old (and modern) *wimpels* are adorned with colorful images such as animals, birds, astrological signs and scenes like a bride and groom under the *chuppah* and the *sefer Torah.*

CHAPTER 31

Bar Mitzvah & Bat Mitzvah

Bar and Bat Mitzvah are Jewish coming of age rituals. *Bar* (Aramaic) or *Ben* (Hebrew) mean 'son'. *Bat* means girl. *Mitzvah* is a commandment and a law.

According to Jewish Law, at the age of 13 a Jewish boy becomes accountable for his actions. Thus, he becomes a *Bar Mitzvah* (plural: *B'nai Mitzvah*). For girls this is at the age of 12. The ages were selected because they roughly coincide with puberty.

In ancient times, puberty was defined as the appearance of two pubic hairs (*simanim*, 'signs'). Puberty in women begins earlier than in men.

Scholars believe that the ceremonial observation of a *Bar Mitzvah* at the age of 13 developed in the Middle Ages.

According to Rabbi Eleazar,*"Until the thirteenth year it is the father's duty to train his boy; after this he must say: "Blessed be He who has taken from me the responsibility [the punishment] for this boy!" "*

Young men who have reached the *bar mitzvah* age can be counted for a *minyan**. They also may lead prayer and other religious services in the family and the community.

Many synagogues require pre-*bar mitzvah* children to attend a minimum number of *Shabbat* prayer services at the synagogue, take on a charity or be active in a community project.

On the first *Shabbat* of his thirteenth year, a Jewish boy is called up to read from the weekly portion of the Law (five books of Moses). In non-orthodox synagogues, girls also can be called up.

GIRL

Between the age of 3-12, called a ***Ketanah*** (minor)

From 12-121/2 called a ***Na'arah*** (young woman)

After 121/2 becomes a ***Bogeret*** (adult)

BOY

3-13 + 1 day: ***Katan*** (minor)

13 + 2 days: becomes a ***Gadol*** (adult)

B'nai Mitzvah festivities typically include a festive meal with family, friends, and members of the community. Some people take their child on a special trip, or organize some special event in the celebrant's honor.

Today, most non-Orthodox Jews celebrate a girl's *Bat Mitzvah* in the same way as a boy's *Bar Mitzvah*. The event is celebrated in style, with a festive meal and many guests. The *Bat Mitzvah* girl gives a speech, receives presents and a blessing from the teacher or rabbi.

Traditional *bar/bat mitzvah* gifts are books with religious or educational value, and religious items. In recent times, cash gifts in multiples of 18 have become the norm. (The numerical equivalent of the Hebrew word for "life", (*chai*), is 18.)

Often, the *Bar Mitzvah* receives his first *tallit** (prayer shawl) from his parents to be used for the occasion. Orthodox families buy their son *tefillin**.

Jewelry is a common gift for a *Bat Mitzvah* girl. Because it is the duty and honor of the woman to light the *Shabbat* candles, a religious *Bat Mitzvah* usually receives a pair of candlesticks.

Over 40% of Jewish families in Israel and many of the Diaspora, prefer to celebrate their son's *Bar Mitzvah* at Jerusalem's Kotel (Western Wall). These celebrations are usually held on Monday and Thursday morning and can be observed from the Western Wall Plaza. *Bar Mitzvah's* are rarely held on *Shabbat,* because taking pictures or filming is strictly forbidden on that day.

At the Kotel in Jerusalem, it can happen that thirteen-year-olds celebrate their *bar mitzvah* together with men in their seventies or eighties. Unable to have a *bar mitzvah* at the time of the Holocaust, they always longed to one day fulfil their dream. In July 2012, twenty Shoah survivors from Tel Aviv became *bar mitzvah* in an initiative of the Western Wall Heritage Foundation.

A Holocaust Survivor and his grandson both celebraing their Bar-Mitzvah

---

Netilat Yadayim
The Ritual of Washing Hands

Netilat yadayim ("Raising [after ritually washing] the hands"), also known as *Mayim Rishonim*, is the washing of the hands with a cup.
Prior to eating any bread with a meal, this is always done with a blessing.
A blessing is not said after touching objects that convey ritual impurity (such as one's private parts, leather shoes, or a ritually unclean animal or insect, or after paying a visit to a cemetery.

The water also must be poured from a vessel as a human act, on the basis of references in the Bible to this practice, e.g. Elisha pouring water upon the hands of Elijah.

Water should be poured on each hand at least twice.

Halacha (Jewish law) requires that the water used for ritual washing be naturally pure, unused, not contain other substances, and not be discolored.

CHAPTER 32

IDF SWEARING IN CEREMONY AT THE KOTEL

The Israel Defense Forces are a people's army. National military service is mandatory for Jewish men and women over the age of 18. Bedouin and Druze men can also enlist. Exceptions are made on religious, physical or psychological grounds, but most Jewish youngsters want to serve in the army.
Men serve three years and women serve two.

Upon enlistment, all soldiers begin a three month basic training course. During this rigorous process of 'integration' they become soldiers instead of citizens. The swearing in ceremony usually takes place after finishing their basic training course.
Even though many army bases have their own swearing in ceremonies, the ones held at the Kotel are extra special. On such a day, soldiers, extra security personnel and family members crowd the site from early morning till the evening.
In the late afternoon, soldiers begin to line up according to their units, while excited family members, fighting for a place to have a good view, are kept out of the cordoned off area.

Keeping their excitement in check, soldiers stand at attention, ready to swear their loyalty to the IDF and to the State of Israel.

There are several speeches from high ranking officers, an army rabbi, and several songs. During one such occasion, a Colonel addressed the crowd with,
"Today we swear allegiance to defend our homeland and we operate out of this commitment. There is no place more appropriate to swear allegiance than the Kotel, a place that combines the old with the new and expresses the depth of our connection to our homeland."

Standing in front of the Western Wall with the soldiers, their families and the Israeli flags gives many a visitor goose bumps. The highlight of the ceremony begins when the colonel reads in a loud voice,
"I swear to uphold the expectations of my country and army. I swear to give myself without condition to the protection of the State of Israel. I swear to be the best soldier I can be."
In response, one company after another shouts at the top of their voices: *"Ani nishbah! - I swear! "* - three times.

It takes a long time before each soldier has run up to his commander to receive a personal weapon and a Torah or Bible.
The ceremony ends with the singing of *Hatikvah* (The Hope)- the national anthem. Family members, who have travelled to Jerusalem from all over the country, are finally allowed to hug 'their' soldier.

The History of *"Hatikvah"*

Rishon le Zion (First to Zion) was established in 1882, with the help of Edmond de Rothschild. The name of the new settlement had been inspired by a phrase from Isaiah 42:27: *"The first shall say to Zion…"* In honor of the establishment, Rumanian born Naphtali Herz Imber wrote a poem called *"Hatikvah"* – the Hope. Samuel Cohen, one of the farmers, set it to music.

On September 1st, 1939, the beginning of the Second World-War, a ship carrying 'illegal' immigrants ran ashore off Tel Aviv. In the glare of the British search lights, the 1,400 refugees on board the cargo ship began to sing *"Hatikvah"*:

*"As long as deep in the heart,
the soul of a Jew yearns,
and towards the East an eye looks to Zion.
Our hope is not yet lost, the age-old hope,
to return to the land of our fathers,
to the city where David dwelt."*

These so-called "illegals", escaping from the Nazis, were interned by the British in the Sarafand Prison camp, northwest of present day Ramla.

During World War II, the British continued their best to keep the desperate Jewish refugees from entering Mandate Palestine. Especially during this time *"Hatikvah"* became symbolic for the longing of the Jewish people for their eternal Promised Land – Zion.

"Hatikvah" officially became the national anthem during the inauguration ceremony of the State of Israel on May 14, 1948. Added to it was a second verse:

"Our hope is not yet lost, the hope of 2,000 years, to be a free people in our land the land of Zion and Jerusalem."

Today, *"Hatikvah"* is still sung with fervor, and its melody and words continue to stir the emotions of both Jews and Christian Zionists.

FAST DAYS OF THE JEWISH CALENDAR

DATE	NAME	REASON	HOW OBSERVED
3 Tishri	Fast of Gedaliah	Commemoration assassination of Gedaliah (2 Kings 25:25)	Dawn to dusk
10 Tishri	Day of Atonement	Atonement for sins (Leviticus 26-32, etc)	Dusk to dusk
10 Tevet	*Asarah be-Tevet*	Nebuchadnezzar besieges Jerusalem (2 Kings 25:1)	Dawn to dusk
13 Adar	Fast of Esther	Traditionally connected with fast-day decreed by Esther (Esther 4:16)	Dawn to dusk
14 Nisan	Fast of the First-born	Commemorates last of the ten plagues (Exodus 12:29)	Dawn to dusk*
17 Tam-muz	*Shivah Asar be-Tammuz*	Associated with breaches of walls of Jerusalem by Nebuchadnezzar (Jeremiah 39:2)	Dawn to dusk
9 Av	*Tisha be-Av*	Associated with Destruction of Temple (2 Kings 25:8-9)	Dusk to dusk

* This fast is usually cancelled by participation in joyful conclusion of study of a Talmudic Tractate.

JEWISH EXPRESSIONS

"Ad meah ve'esrim!" May you live to 120! (Because Moses lived to 120.)

"Be ezrat haShem!" Lit. with the help of the name [of God], or God willing.   *B"H*   ב"ה

Besiyata Dishmaya (Aramaic) - with the help of Heaven. Even though the acronym is not mentioned   בס"ד *BS"D*   in the *Halacha*, it is widely used at the top of written documents. We are to be reminded that all comes from God, and that without God's help we can do nothing of eternal value.

BIKKUR CHOLIM - Visiting the Sick

A major commandment in Jewish tradition is to visit and comfort the sick and to attend to their needs. According to the Talmud, visiting a sick person takes away 1/60 of his sickness, while failing to do so may lead to the sick person's death.

Rabbi Eleazar the Great wrote: *"My son, pay careful attention to visiting the sick, because one who visits him lessens his illness. Entreat him to return to his Creator, and pray for him, and then leave. Let not your presence b a burden to him, because he has enough of a burden with his illness. When you go to visit a person who is sick, enter joyfully, because his eyes and heart are directed to those who enter to visit him."*

GLOSSARY

ADAR - the sixth month of the civil year and the twelfth month of the ecclesiastical year on the Hebrew calendar.

ALIYAH - (Lit. going up.) During synagogue service, a man is honoured to go up on the bimah to recite a blessing over the Torah. Aliyah is also the word that describes the return of the Jewish People from the exile in the Diaspora back to the Land of Israel. The word is derived from the verb "la'alot" - "to go up", or "to ascend" in a positive spiritual sense. A person who makes Aliyah is called an Oleh, meaning "one who goes up". The opposite action, emigration from Israel, is referred to as yerida -"descent".

ANINUT - First stage of mourning, when someone is in shock, and disoriented.

ARBA'AH NIMIM - "Four Species", waved during Sukkot.

ARK (Torah) in a synagogue. Aron Kodesh by the Ashkenazim; Hekhál amongst most Sephardim. Oftn an ornamental closet, which contains the Torah scrolls.

ASHKENAZI(M) - Jewish descendants from the medieval communities along the Rhine in Germany, from Alsace (south) to the Rhineland (north).

AUFRUF - Yiddish for 'calling up'), is the custom to call up a groom for an aliyah. Ashkenazim hold the ceremony on the Shabbat before the wedding, while Sephardim hold it on the Shabbat after the wedding.

AV - the eleventh month of the civil year and the fifth month of the ecclesiastical year on the Hebrew calendar. The name is Babylonian in origin and appeared in the Talmud around the 3rd century. This is the only month which is not named in the Bible. Av usually occurs in July–August.

AVELUT - Mourning stage after the funeral. One year for a direct family members; 30 days for second degree family.

AVODAH - ("service" and "worship"). During Temple times it described the order of service for the High priest on Yom Kippur. In modern Hebrew, avodah means work. Work is service AND worship.

BASHERT - Yiddish for "destiny", and often used in the context of one's divinely foreordained spouse or soul mate.

BASHOW - (sit in). Prospective bridegroom and his parents visit the young woman in her house to see if the prospective couple are compatible.

BAR/BAT MITSVAH - Jewish coming-of-age ceremonies; girls at the age of 12, boys at the age of 13.

BAYIT KEVAROT - (BAYIT OLAM) - Jewish cemetery.

BAYIT MIDRASH - synagogue or yeshiva study hall.

BIKKUR CHOLIM - (Visiting the sick) A major commandment in Jewish tradition is to visit and comfort the sick and to attend to their needs.

BIMAH or tebah (Sephardic) - the elevated area or platform in a synagogue which is intended to serve the place where the person reading aloud from the Torah stands during the Torah reading service.

Birkat HaMazon (Grace after Meals, Benshen in Yiddish) - recited at the end of the festive meal to thank God for the food and sustenance that has been enjoyed.

CHALLAH - Jewish braided bread eaten on Sabbath and holidays.

CHAMETZ - is any food product made from wheat, barley, rye, oats, spelt, or their derivatives, which has leavened (risen) or fermented; forbidden to eat during the seven days of the Pesach holiday.

CHAMSA - popular palm-shaped amulet, commonly used in jewelry and wall hangings. The open right hand, used as a sign of protection, is believed to provide defense against the evil eye. Also known as the hand of Fatima (Mohammed's daughter).

CHANUKAH - eight-day Jewish holiday commemorating the rededication of the Second Temple in Jerusalem at the time of the Maccabean Revolt of the 2nd century BC. Chanukah is observed for eight nights and days, starting on the 25th day of Kislev; may occur from late November to late December in the Gregorian calendar.

CHANUKIAH - candelabrum with eight candle holders with an elevated 9th, lit during the Chanukah festival.

CHASSIDIM (Hassidim; Ultra-Orthodox Jews) - A Hassidic dynasty usually takes its name from the town in Eastern Europe where it was based; You'll find many diverse groups, following "their" Rabbi. This stream of Judaism demands that every Hassid personally participates in the dissemination of Torah and Judaism to one's surroundings and seek out the benefit of one's fellow Jews.

CHATAN - bridegroom

CHATAN BERESHIT - bridegroom of Genesis; the man called to recite or chant the blessings over the first section of the Torah on Simchat Torah.

CHATAN TORAH - the man called to recite or chant the blessings over the final section of the Torah on Simchat Torah.

CHAZZAN - Jewish cantor, a musician trained in the vocal arts who helps lead the congregation in songful prayer.

CHESHVAN - (lit. "eighth month"), the second month of the civil Jewish year (which starts on 1 Tishrei) and the eighth month of the ecclesiastical year (which starts on 1 Nisan) on the Hebrew calendar.

CHEVRAH KEDISHA - Jewish burial society.

CHOL HAMOED - lit. weekday; mundane), the intermediate days of Pesach and Sukkot.

CHUPPAH - (lit. "canopy" or "covering") is a canopy under which a bride and groom stand during their wedding ceremony. It consists of a cloth or sheet, (sometimes tallit), stretched or supported over four poles. Sometimes friends of the groom hold up the poles. A chuppah symbolizes the home that the couple will build together.

COHEN - a male descendant of Aaron, the brother of Moses. Being a Cohen is associated with certain privileges and religious obligations.

COMMANDMENTS (613) - religious Jews are commanded to keep. Of the 613, 365 are negative (prohibited), corresponding with the days of the solar year; the 248 positive (duties to perform) are linked to the number of limbs in the human body.

DAVENEN (davnen) - Yiddish word for praying - widely used by Ashkenazim.

DIASPORA (Greek for 'scattering', 'dispersion') - the movement, migration or scattering of people away from an estabished or ancestral homeland. The word has come to refer to historical mass-dispersions of people with common roots, particularly movements of an involuntary nature, such as the expulsion of Jews from the Middle East. Even though the Jewish people often found themselves separated from their national territory, they always kept hoping to return to their homeland. In this book, 'diaspora' refers to Jews living outside Eretz Yisrael.

DREIDEL - see SEVIVON

ELUL- twelfth month of the Jewish civil year and the sixth month of the ecclesiastical year on the Hebrew calendar. Usually August–September.

ERETZ YISRAEL - a name for the territory roughly corresponding to the area encompassed by the Southern Levant (Canaan); Roman Judea was called *Palestina;* also called the Promised Land [after the Biblical promise of land to Abraham and his offspring]; sometimes also called the Holy Land.

EZRAT NASHIM - Separate prayer area for women. The original *ezrat nashim* was located in the eastern sector of the court of the Second.

FASTING and FAST DAYS - in Jewish tradition are a religious discipline involving abstention from food, drink and physical pleasures for the purpose of the intensifying spiritual experience in atonement for sin. Fasting takes place when commemorating national tragedies or as part of a personal petition to God in seeking His help.

FESTIVALS AND *YOM TOV'S* - "Yom tov' literally means 'a good day'. Biblical Law ordains seven festival days upon which work is prohibited - *Rosh haShana, Yom Kippur, Sukkot, Shemini Atseret,* the first and last day of *Pesach and Shavuot.*

FIRST TEMPLE PERIOD - 1006-586 BCE

GALUT - (Golus) lit. exile- referring to the (four) exiles of the Jewish people from the Land of Israel.

***GARTEL* -** (Yiddish, belt; German, Gürtel), is a girdle worn by Chassidim during prayer.

GEMARAH - (Gemorah) means "to complete", and is part of the Talmud. The terms Gemarah and Talmud usually refer to the Babylonian versions.

GENIZAH - a storeroom for worn-out and damaged holy manuscripts and books, as well as ritual objects such as tefillin or mezuzot. By Jewish Law, such items cannot be thrown out as trash, but must be disposed of in a reverential manner. This usually means burying the items in the local Jewish cemetery. Until this takes place, many synagogues have a chest or room they use as a genizah, which literally means "storage".

HAKHEL - custom based on the mandated practice of assembling all Jewish men, women and children to hear the reading of the Torah by the king of Israel once every seven years.

HAFDALAH - ceremony marking the end of Shabbat and holidays; it ushers in the beginning of the new week.

HAFTARAH - (Lit. conclusion.) A reading from the Prophets, read along with the weekly Torah portion.

HAGADDAH - Jewish text that sets forth the order of the Passover Seder. Reading the Haggadah at the Seder table is a fulfillment of the commandment to each Jew to "tell your son" of the Jewish liberation from slavery in Egypt. (Exodus 13:8).

HAKAFFOT - (lit. "going around in circles") the sevenfold dancing procession made with the Torah scrolls on the holiday of Simchat Torah.

HALACHA - Jewish law and jurisprudence, based on the Talmud.

HALLEL - A portion of the service for certain Jewish festivals; (Psalms 113–118)

HAZKARAH - last memorial service of the first 12 months of mourning.

HEFKER - any fruits which grow of their own accord are deemed ownerless and may be picked by anyone.

HECHAL - ark in which the Torah scrolls are kept.

HIGH HOLY DAYS - (*Yamim Noraim* - "Days of Awe") are Rosh Hashana (Jewish New Year) and Yom Kippur.

HOSHANA RABAH - Seventh day of the Jewish holiday of Sukkot, 21st day of Tishrei.

ISRU CHAG - (lit. "Bind the Festival") the day after Pesach, Shavuot and Sukkot.

IYAR - the eighth month of the civil year; the second month of the ecclesiastical year. Usually in April and May.

KABBALAH - The ancient Jewish tradition of mystical interpretation of the Bible, first transmitted orally and using esoteric methods.

***KABBALAT PANIM* -** (lit. "Greeting of Faces") is the opening reception of a wedding.

KABBALAT SHABBAT - (lit. Receiving of Shabbat), a mystical ritual designed to welcome Shabbat.

KADDISH - (Lit. sanctification) is an Aramaic prayer of praise to God. A prayer in synagogue and recited by mourners.

KALLAH - Jewish bride

KETUBAH - marriage contract between a husband and wife that is signed before a Jewish wedding.

KERIAH - the practice of rending or cutting a garment, or symbolically wearing a cut black ribbon over the heart, as a sign of mourning.

KETUVIM - (Writings) Poetic Books: Psalms, Proverbs, Job; Five Megillot: Song of Songs, Ruth, Lamentations, Ecclesiastes, Esther; Other: Daniel, Ezra - Nehemiah, Chronicles

KEVURAH - Jewish burial.

KIDDUSH - (lit. sanctification) a blessing recited over wine (or grape juice) to sanctify the Shabbat, Jewish holidays, or special events.

KIDDUSH LEVANAH - sanctification of the new moon (Rosh Chodesh).

KISLEV - Third month of the civil and ninth of the religious year. Usually in November and December.

KITTEL (Yiddish) - a white robe worn by Ashkenazim on special occasions (Yom Kippur, Rosh haShana and during the Passover Seder). Orthodox men wear a kittel on their wedding day, and also serves as a burial shroud for men. Because Isaiah 1:18 says, "Our sins shall be made as white as snow", a kittel is always white.

KOL NIDREI - both the opening prayer and the name for the evening service that begins Yom Kippur.

KOSHER/ KASHER - fit or proper in the context of food that can be eaten according to traditional Jewish law. The pig has become the most notable symbol of the non-kosher animal.

LAG BAOMER - Thirty-third day in the period of the counting of the 'omer ("Lag" = 33), corresponding to the 18th day of Iyyar.

LULAV - Four species (Sukkot) together.

MACHZOR - the prayer book used by Jews on the High Holidays of Rosh Hashanah and Yom Kippur.

MAFTIR - the last person called to the Torah on Shabbat and holiday mornings: this person also reads the haftarah portion.

MAPPAH - see wimpel

MATSAH - unleavened bread traditionally eaten by Jews during the week-long Pesach holiday.

MENORAH - a seven-branched lamp-stand used in the ancient Tabernacle in the desert and Temple in Jerusalem

MEZUZAH - A parchment inscribed with religious texts and attached in a case to the doorpost of a Jewish house as a sign of faith.

MIKVEH (Mikvah) a bath used for the purpose of ritual immersion. Lit."a collection of water".

MA'ARIV - evening prayers.

MECHITSAH - (Halachic) partition, used to separate men and women.

MEGILLAH - One of five books of the Hebrew scriptures (the Song of Solomon, Ruth, Lamentations, Ecclesiastes, and Esther).

MIDRASH - a method of exegesis of a Biblical text, but can also be a compilation of teachings and commentaries on the Tenach.

MIKVAH/MIKVEH - Ritual bath.

MINCHAH - afternoon prayers.

MINYAN - (lit. to count, number) quorum of ten Jewish men required for prayer services.

MISHLOACH MANOT - Gift basket with sweets and wine given during Purim.

MISHNAH - The Hebrew root of the word means "to repeat", and refers to memorization by repetition. Mishnah can refer to the tradition of the Oral Torah, which was formulated in the first centuries AD.

MITZVAH - a good (charitable) deed performed out of religious duty, or a precept or commandment of the Jewish law.

MOHEL - a Jewish person trained in the practice of a Brit Milah (circumcision).

MUSAF - an additional service that is recited on Shabbat, Yom Tov, Chol Hamoed, and Rosh Chodesh

NE'ILAH - last of the five services held on the Day of Atonement.

NER ZIKARON - memorial candle which burns 24 hours.

NEVI'IM - Bible books (O.T): Joshua, Judges, Samuel, Kings, Isaiah, Jeremiah, Ezekiel;
Hosea, Joel, Amos, Jonah, Obadiah, Micha, Nahum, Habakkuk, Zephaniah, Haggai, Zechariah, Malachi.

NIDDAH - a woman who is menstruating, or has menstruated, and still is perceived 'unclean', until she has been to the mikveh.

NISAN - seventh month of the civil and first of the religious year, usually March and April.

OMER - An ancient Hebrew dry measure, the tenth part of an ephah or a sheaf of corn or omer of grain presented as an offering on the second day of Pesach.

ORAL LAW - a legal commentary on the Torah (written Law) which explains how its commandments are to be carried out.

ORTHODOX - Jew who practices strict observance of Mosaic law.

PILGRIM FESTIVALS - known as the *Shalosh Regalim* are three major festivals in Judaism — *Pesach (Passover), Shavuot (Weeks), and Sukkot* (Feast of Tabernacles).

PURIM - lesser Jewish festival held in spring (on the 14th or 15th day of Adar) to commemorate the defeat of Haman's plot to massacre the Jews.

RA'ASHAN - gregger, used to make noise while in synagogue the name "Haman" is read.

RABBI - Jewish scholar or teacher, esp. one who studies or teaches Jewish law. Or a person appointed as a Jewish religious leader.

REFORM - liberal Jew who tries to adapt all aspects of Judaism to modern circumstances

ROSH HASHANAH - Jewish New Year. It falls once a year during the month of Tishrei and occurs ten days before Yom Kippur.

ROSH CHODESH - the beginning of each month in the Jewish calendar; marked by a special liturgy.

SAGE - wise, old man, spiritual teacher, religious leader, often paternal figure.

SANDEK - Man honoured to hold the baby during his circumcision.

SANHEDRIN - (lit." sitting together," hence "assembly" or "council") in Bible times, an assembly of twenty-three judges appointed in every city in the Land of Israel. Presently, the highest court of justice and the supreme council in ancient Jerusalem.

SECOND TEMPLE PERIOD - Jewish history in Judea lasted between 530 BCE and 70 CE, when the Second Temple of Jerusalem was destroyed by the Romans.

SEDER - Jewish ritual service and ceremonial dinner for the first night or first two nights of Passover.

SEGULA - a kind of talisman (like the Kabbalistic red string), to ward off misfortune against the 'evil eye'.

SEFER TORAH - "Book(s) of Torah" or "Torah scroll (s)") - a handwritten copy of the Torah or Pentateuch.

SEPHARDI(M) - general term referring to the descendants of Spanish-Portuguese Jews who lived in the Iberian Peninsula before being expelled in 1492. Also a style of liturgy.

SEPTUAGINT - (or "LXX", or "Greek Old Testament") is a translation of the Hebrew Bible and some related texts into Greek, begun in the late 3rd century BCE.

SEVIVON - Dreidel. Chanukah toy.

SHABBAT HAGADOL - Shabbat before Pesach.

SHACHARIT - is the daily morning Tefillah (prayer) of the Jewish people, one of the three times there is prayer each day.

SHADCHAN - Matchmaker. Also a stapler in Hebrew.

SHAMASH - 9th candle in the Chanukiah, used to light the other 8 candles.

SHAVUOT - the Festival of Weeks, is the second of the three major festivals with both historical and agricultural significance (the other two are Pesach and Sukkot.

SHECHITAH - kosher slaughtering of animals, performed by a professional called a shochet. This form of slaughtering strives to minimize the pain experienced by the animal.

SHEKINAH - The glory of the divine presence, conventionally represented as light.

SHEMA - A Hebrew text consisting of three passages from the Pentateuch and beginning "Hear, O Israel, the Lord is our God, the Lord is one."

SHEMINI ATZERET - "the Eighth [day] of Assembly"; celebrated on the 22nd day of the Hebrew month of Tishrei.

SHMITAH - Sabbatical year.

SHEMIRAT NEGIAH - Halacha - forbidden or restricted physical contact with a member of the opposite sex.

SEUDAT HAVRA'AH - The first meal eaten by the mourners when they return home from the funeral; the meal of recovery or condolence.

SHEVA BRACHOT (seven blessings) - recited both under the chuppah and at the end of the wedding dinner. Also the name of the seven invitations the newly-weds receive to have dinner with friends.

SHEVAT - the fifth month of the civil year and the eleventh month of the ecclesiastical year on the Hebrew calendar. Usually January–February.

SHIDDUCH - a match resulting in marriage.

SHIVA - Seven mourning days after the funeral.

SHLOSHIM - end of 30 day mourning period.

SHOFAR - an instrument made from the horn of a ram or other kosher animal. It was used in ancient Israel to announce the Rosh Chodesh (New Moon) and call people together. It was also blown on Rosh Hashanah, the Jewish New Year. Connected to the Binding of Isaac (Genesis 22) in which Abraham sacrifices a ram in place of his son, Isaac.

SHOMER - Jewish legal guardian, entrusted with the custody and care of another person.

SHULCHAN ARUCH - (lit. "Set Table") also known as the Code of Jewish Law - the most authoritative legal code of (Sephardic) Judaism. Compiled in Safed in 1563, it was published two years later in Venice, Italy.

SIDDUR - Jewish prayer book, containing a set order of daily prayers.

SIMCHAT TORAH - marks the completion of the annual Torah reading cycle and is one of the most joyous holidays on the Jewish calendar.

SIVAN - third of the twelve months of the Jewish calendar. The month in which God descended on Mt. Sinai and gave the Torah to the Jewish people.

SIYUM - the completion of any unit of Torah study, or book of the Mishnah or Talmud.

SUFGANIAH - (Jelly) filled donuts eaten during Chanukah.

SUKKAH - Booth during the Feast of Tabernacles.

SUKKOT - Feast of Tabernacles. Third Pilgrim Festival.

TALLIT - Jewish prayer shawl, traditionally made of wool, worn over the outer clothes during morning prayers. Attached to its four corners are tzitzit, special twined and knotted fringes.

TALLIT KATAN - a fringed undergarment worn by Orthodox, Chassidic and some Conservative Jewish males.

TALMUD a record of rabbinic discussions in connection to the Jewish Law, ethics, customs and history. It contains two parts: Mishnah (200 AD) – oral law and Gemarah (500 AD) – further discussion, expounds broadly on the Tenach.

TAMMUZ - fourth month of the Jewish calendar.

TARGUM - An ancient Aramaic paraphrase or interpretation of the Hebrew Bible

TASHLICH - ceremony held on the first day of Rosh Hashanah. People symbolically cast their sins into the water of a lake, river or in the sea.

TENA'IM - betrothal documents similar to an engagement contract, agreed upon and signed by two representatives.

TENACH - an abbreviation of Torah, Nevi'im - (Prophets) and Ketuvim (Writings).

TEFILLIN - two small black boxes with black straps attached to them; Jewish men are required to place one box on their head and tie the other one on their arm.

TENACH - abbreviation of: Torah; Nevi'im - Prophets; Ketuvim – Writings

TEVET - the tenth in the number of months counting from Nisan. The name was acquired in Babylonia.

TISHA BE'AV - a Jewish day of mourning - and a fast day - that commemorates the destruction of the two Temples.

TISHRI - (or Tishrei) first month of the civil year (which starts on 1 Tishrei) and the seventh month of the ecclesiastical year (which starts on 1 Nisan).

TORAH - first five books of the *Tenach* (Hebrew Bible) or the Old Testament.

TOSAFOT - medieval commentaries on the Talmud

TOSEFTA - (lit. Additions, Supplements) a compilation of the Jewish oral law from the period of the Mishnah.

TZADDIK - a title given to personalities who in Jewish tradition are considered to be righteous.

TZEDAKAH - Charitable giving, typically seen as a moral obligation.

TSITSIT - specially knotted ritual fringes worn by observant Jews. Attached to the four corners of the tallit (prayer shawl) and tallit katan.

TZENIUT - modest behaviour between unmarried/ unrelated men and women.

TU BE'SHVAT - minor Jewish holiday, occurring on the 15th day of the Hebrew month of Shevat.

UPSHERIN - Ceremony of cutting the hair of 3 year old Jewish boys during Lag Ba'Omer.

USHPEZIN - (Aramaic for 'guests') seven mystical guests who visit the sukkah during Sukkot: Abraham, Isaac, Jacob, Joseph, Moses, Aaron and David. It became customary to invite a needy Yeshiva student to sit at the head of the table to deputize for the special ushpezin guest of that evening. This custom continues to be practiced by many ultra-orthodox and Chassidic Jews.

WIMPEL - a long, linen sash that German Jews used as a cover for the Sefer Torah. It was made from the cloth used to swaddle a baby boy at his Brith milah.

YAD - Pointer used to follow the text from a Torah scroll.

YAMIM NORA'IM - High Holy Days; Days of Awe; period between *Rosh haShana and Yom Kippur.*

YESHIVA - (lit. "sitting") a Jewish educational institution that focuses on the study of traditional religious texts, primarily the Talmud and Torah study.

YICHUD - ritual during the wedding in which the newly married couple spends a period secluded in a room by themselves. In the Talmudic era, the marriage would be consummated at this time, but that practice is no longer current. The term also means the impermissibility of seclusion of a non-related man and a woman in a private area.

YOM KIPPUR - Day of Atonement, the holiest and most solemn day of the year for the Jews. Central themes: atonement and repentance.

YOM TOV - (Lit. "good day") Jewish holiday or festival is a day or series of days observed by Jews as a holy or secular commemoration of an important event.

YOVEL - The Jubilee year is the year at the end of seven cycles of Sabbatical years (*Shmita*)

BIBLIOGRAPHY

- Alexander, Pat (ed). *THE LION ENCYCLOPEDIA OF THE BIBLE*. Oxford: Lion Publishing, 1978. Print.
- Benjamin, Don C., and Victor H. Matthews. *Social World of Ancient Israel: 1250-587 BCE*. Peabody Massachusetts: Hendrickson Publishers, 2005. Print.
- Edersheim, Alfred. *Sketches of Jewish Social Life: Updated Edition*. Peabody Massachusetts: Hendrickson Publishers, 1994. Print.
- Edersheim, Alfred. *Bible History Old Testament: New Updated Edition*. Peabody Massachusetts: Hendrickson Publishers, 1995. Print.
- *Eyewitness Guides: Bible Lands (Collins Eyewitness guides)*. Sydney: Angus & Robertson, 1991. Print.
- Gilbert, Martin. *Israel: a history*. New York: Morrow, 1998. Print.
- Gower, Ralph. *The New Manners & Customs of Bible Times*. Chicago: Moody Publishers, 2005. Print.
- Harold, Victor Matthews;. *Manners and Customs in the Bible*. Peabody, Massachusetts: Hendrickson Publishers Inc, 1991. Print.
- Hudson, Angus. *The world of the Bible*. Carlisle, Cumbria: Candle Books, 1999. Print.
- Hudson, Angus. *Life in Bible times*. Carlisle, Cumbria: Candle Books, 1999. Print.
- K., R., and Harrison. *Old Testament Times: A Social, Political, and Cultural Context*. Grand Rapids, Michigan: Baker Books, 2005. Print.
- Miller, Madeleine S., and John Lane Miller. *Harper's encyclopedia of Bible life*. Third rev. ed. San Francisco: Harper & Row, 1978. Print.
- Renberg, Dalia Hardof. *The complete family guide to Jewish holidays*. New York: Adama Books, 1985. Print.
- S., Madeleine, and J. Lane Miller. *HARPER'S ENCYCLOPEDIA OF BIBLE LIFE*. New York: Harper & Row, 1971. Print.
- SNELL, Daniel C.. *Life in the Ancient Near East: 3100-332 B.C.E*. New York: Yale University Press,, New Haven:, 1997. Print.
- Vamosh, Miriam Feinberg. *Women at the time of the Bible*. Herzlia, Israel: Palphot, 2007. Print.
- Wigoder, Geoffrey. *The Encyclopedia of Judaism*. New York: Macmillan; 1989. Print.
- Internet: Wikipedia; Chabad.org; and misc. websites.

MLA formatting by BibMe.org.